"*Talk the Talk* is packed with all sorts of tools to help the characters breathe, stand up, and come alive."

> — Shawn Lawrence Otto, Screenwriter and Co-Producer, *House of Sand and Fog*

"Put this book in action and see your dialogue leap off the page."

> — Joan Scott, Founder of Writers & Artists Agency and Joan Scott Management

"This is the book dramatic writers have been looking for! Teachers and students alike will find its sound advice and step-by-step approach invaluable and inspiring."

> — Rebecca Gilman, Playwright and Screenwriter; Author of *Spinning into Butter* and *Boy Gets Girl*

"Its discussion of status — its effect on dialogue, and how it shifts in various contexts — is particularly illuminating."

> — Wendy MacLeod, Playwright and Screenwriter; Author of *The House of Yes*, *Schoolgirl Figure*, and *Juvenilia.*

"Hollywood wants great scripts. Great scripts must have great dialogue. Great dialogue writing begins with this book."

> — Brantley M. Dunaway, Producer, *Love in the Time of Cholera*

"*Talk the Talk* opened my eyes to new ways of looking at developing characters and their dialogue. Highly recommended for course work or for the individual."

> — Paul Chitlik, Author of *Rewrite: A Step-by-Step Guide to Strengthen Structure, Characters, and Drama in Your Screenplay*

"Although *Talk the Talk* is a must-read for student and aspiring screenwriters, it also should be heralded as a fantastic resource for professionals. The exercises are simple, yet thought-provoking, and are easily adjusted for television, film or theatre. *Talk the Talk* will certainly help writers of all levels break free of old ruts and look at dialogue in a fresh, dynamic, creative way!"

> — Steve Baldikoski, Television Writer and Producer, *Glenn Martin, DDS*; *8 Simple Rules for Dating My Teenage Daughter*; *Andy Richter Controls the Universe*

"Thorough, thought-out and extremely helpful... this book will make your dialogue explode off the page."
— Matthew Terry, Filmmaker, Screenwriter, Teacher; Columnist for *www.hollywoodlitsales.com*

"*Talk the Talk* will help you determine which characters should be allowed to speak and what they should say, depending on their importance to your story."
— Mary J. Schirmer, Screenwriter, Writing Instructor, Film Critic

"*Talk the Talk* is an accessible and wonderfully helpful book. Full of exercises, examples, and great advice, this book illuminates why, where and when dialogue is needed."
— Jule Selbo, Screenwriter; Associate Professor, Lead of Screenwriting Program, California State University, Fullerton

"*Talk the Talk* is a perfect gem of a book that directly addresses the daunting challenge of writing dialogue that works. It should be a prerequisite for every writer's library, whether you're tackling a novel, play, or script."
— Kathie Fong Yoneda, Script Consultant, Workshop Leader, Author of *The Script-Selling Game: A Hollywood Insider's Look at Getting Your Script Sold and Produced*

"Whether you're writing comedy or drama, movies or plays, even novels and short stories — *Talk the Talk* is a must-have workout for the imagination."
— Chad Gervich. TV Writer/Producer; Author, *Small Screen, Big Picture: A Writer's Guide to the TV Business*

"As Penniston states in the book's introduction, 'Great moments of dialogue are the great moments of film and theater.' With this workshop, you'll learn to create your own insightful, original dialogues that will give your writing a competitive edge. What are you waiting for?"
— Amanda Porter, Associate Editor, *School Video News*

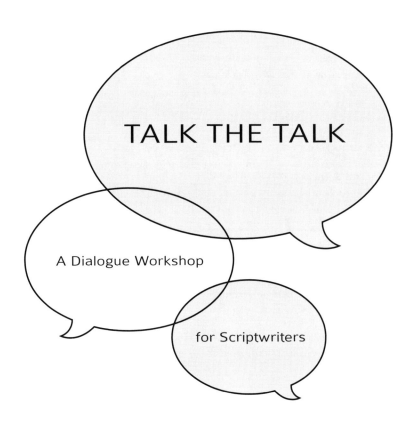

TALK THE TALK

A Dialogue Workshop

for Scriptwriters

PENNY PENNISTON

MICHAEL WIESE PRODUCTIONS

Published by Michael Wiese Productions
3940 Laurel Canyon Blvd. – Suite 1111
Studio City, CA 91604
(818) 379-8799, (818) 986-3408 (FAX)
mw@mwp.com
www.mwp.com

Cover design by MWP
Interior design by William Morosi
Edited by Gary Sunshine
Printed by McNaughton & Gunn

Manufactured in the United States of America
Copyright 2009

Library of Congress Cataloging-in-Publication Data
ISBN 978-1-932907-70-4
Penniston, Penny, 1970-
Talk the talk : a dialogue workshop for scriptwriters / Penny Penniston.
    p. cm.
ISBN 978-1-932907-70-4
1. Motion picture authorship. 2. Television authorship. 3. Drama--Technique. 4. Dialogue. I. Title.
PN1996.P46 2010
808'.066791--dc22

                                   2009029892

Mixed Sources
Product group from well-managed forests and other controlled sources
www.fsc.org Cert no. SW-COC-002283
© 1996 Forest Stewardship Council
FSC

CONTENTS

Dialogue: How People Talk to Each Other

GEORGE: My mother thanks you. My father thanks you. My sister thanks you. And I thank you.
—*Yankee Doodle Dandy* (1942)

Acknowledgments

Thanks to Dave Bell, Jessica Ross, and Kathy Stieber for allowing me to raid their DVD collections. Thanks to Kathleen Lange for her assistance in compiling the dialogue quotes that begin each chapter. Finally, I am grateful to Michael Wiese, Ken Lee, and Gary Sunshine for their guidance in putting this book together.

This book was born out of my experience teaching Dramatic Writing at Northwestern University. With warm wishes, I dedicate it to all of my former students. Keep writing.

HENRY: Words if you look after them... they can build bridges.

—Tom Stoppard (*The Real Thing*)

Introduction

WHY YOU NEED THIS BOOK

Dialogue puts conversation in motion. Great dialogue moves like a great athlete; it is nimble, precise, and powerful. It commands the attention, yet feels effortless in its execution. However, if we want our dialogue to move like an athlete, then we must train like an athlete.

This is a book of exercises to tone the scriptwriter's dialogue skills. It is written for university-level playwriting and screenwriting students or preprofessional writing groups and workshops. It is also appropriate for professional playwrights and screenwriters who wish to keep their dialogue skills sharp.

Most playwriting and screenwriting books take a sweeping scope. They tend to include a brief discussion of dialogue, but then abandon the topic in favor of other issues. *Talk the Talk* is exclusively a focused examination of and an exercise regimen for dialogue writing. By mastering this fundamental building block of dramatic writing, authors breathe life into characters and create scripts that jump off the page. Great moments of dialogue are the great moments of film and theater.

HOW TO USE THIS BOOK

This book is based on a few core beliefs about the teaching of writing:

Writers Learn by Writing

The frustrating thing about dialogue writing is that it seems like it ought to be easy. We all engage in dialogue every day. We've all been in situations that are funny or ironic or tragic. And, being human and living in a world of humans, we are all experts on human behavior. So why is it so hard?

The truth is that all those things are just the notes of drama. They are the keys on the piano. Anyone can come along and make noise on a piano – all you have to do is bang on the keys. But to make music on a piano – that is harder. It requires striking a particular set of notes in a particular sequence in order to generate a particular set of sounds. Trained pianists do this gracefully and beautifully. Their fingers glide across the keys. They make it look effortless. The truth is that it only got to be effortless after lots and lots of practice.

So if you want to be a writer, practice writing. Practice it the way a musician practices her instrument. Great piano players did not become great by attending lectures and reading books on music theory. Those things certainly helped, but, at the end of the day, it is years and years of fingers on the keyboard that make a piano player. Scales and drills and études get played over and over again until they become instinctive. Technique that once required careful concentration becomes effortless and subliminal. It is the same with writing. Think of this book as a book of scales and études. Use this book to drill technique into your muscle memory so that when you sit down at your keyboard in the future, the dialogue will flow effortlessly.

A few tips on doing the exercises in this book:

There are twenty lessons in this book. Most lessons contains four dialogue-writing exercises. These exercises are marked in the margins so that you can find them easily:

- Script Analysis Exercises are marked with a ●.
- Beginner Exercises are marked with a ▲.
- Intermediate/Advanced Exercises are marked with a ■.
- Solo Exercises are marked with a ✚.

All exercises are appropriate for both screenwriters and playwrights. However, if you are focusing exclusively on screenwriting or exclusively on playwriting, then I recommend the following tweaks to the exercises:

- When doing the script analysis exercises, screen-writers should exclusively analyze films. Playwrights should exclusively analyze stage plays. (The Appendix includes script suggestions for both film and theater.)
- Screenwriters should write all dialogue in standard screenplay format. Playwrights should write all dialogue in standard playscript format.
- In general, screenplays have shorter dialogue scenes than stage plays. Therefore, when doing a dialogue-writing exercise, screenwriters should lean toward the lower end of the recommended page count. Playwrights should lean toward the higher end of the recommended page count.

The Best Feedback Is from an Audience

As playwrights and screenwriters, we aren't just writing, we are writing for an audience. Writing without an audience is simply a form of self-expression. We write down all sorts of things for our own reference: lists, notes for class, journal entries, etc. This writing exists only for ourselves. We don't expect or require other people to take meaning from it.

Writing for an audience is different. We write something and an audience interprets it. It is an act of communication. If we do our job well, the meaning that we put into our words will interact constructively with the meaning that the audience takes from our words. Or, to put it simply: Our audience will understand what the hell we are talking about.

As writers, it's easy to lose sight of the audience. We assume that, if we understand what is happening in the story and what we are trying to communicate with the story, then surely an audience will understand it as well. We know our story and our intent so well that we lose the perspective of someone who is experiencing our script for the first time.

Therefore, one of the most useful ways to hone your craft is to get feedback from others. You need people to act as your audience – people who can give you objective feedback about the effect your writing is having upon them. Is it clear? Is it coherent? Does it move them? Does it engage them? These are hard questions to answer on your own. You need a group setting: a classroom, a workshop, or a writers' group.

Most of the exercises in this book are designed for this kind of environment. I encourage you to find trusted peers to help evaluate your work. This might be easier in a large city, but, thanks to the Internet, no one has to be excluded from forming his or her own support group of fellow writers. Once you have completed the group exercises in each chapter, you can do the solo exercises on your own as a regular writer's workout.

If you are truly on your own, then you must develop the ability to be your own audience. This means putting your completed work away for a few weeks and then reviewing it as if you were a virgin to the material. You can still go through the discussion questions, but you must split your perspective in half. Debate the discussion questions between two sides of yourself: the writer and the objective audience-member.

There Are Only Two Kinds of Writing Advice

From your point of view, there is not good advice or bad advice. There is not right advice and wrong advice. There is only:

- Helpful Advice
- Not Helpful Advice

Making this distinction forces you to take responsibility for figuring out what you need, right now, to make your work better and to help you along in this moment. It also keeps your work and your artistic ego from getting torn apart in the endless crosscurrents of opinions from teachers, professionals, and peers.

So… read books on writing. Attend lectures on writing. Take writing classes and workshops. Try out everything that anyone suggests. If you find a suggestion helpful, use it. If it's not helpful, ignore it for the moment – just keep working with the helpful stuff; keep writing. In six months, revisit the unhelpful advice. Reevaluate it. Maybe it's helpful now. Maybe you're at a different place in your writing. Maybe the advice that was completely useless and 100% not helpful six months ago is now suddenly, miraculously… brilliant. If that's the case, use it. If that's not the case, ignore it for six more months, then evaluate it again. Is it helpful yet? If so, use it; if not, put it aside for six more months. Repeat this process over and over again until you die. By the sheer force of evolution, the useful advice will end up in your work and the useless advice will stay out of your way.

Per my own instructions, try out everything in this book. But if any section is, in your opinion, not the thing you need to help you along in this particular moment, then ignore it. Go find the helpful stuff. Go find the useful stuff. Focus on that.

THE VOICE:
HOW PEOPLE TALK

LESSON ONE:
Capturing the Voice

Hamlet

As a scriptwriter, one of the first things you need to master is the ability to capture dialogue on the page. This is trickier than it sounds. Schools spend years drilling us in prose writing – writing that is meant to be read. Dialogue isn't meant to be read; it is meant to be heard. The scriptwriter has the difficult task of taking something that is meant to be heard, putting it on the page in such a way that it can be read, but ultimately making sure that once it comes off the page and into an actor's mouth, it will still sound like speech.

Scriptwriters do this by abandoning almost everything we ever learned about composition, grammar, and

3

punctuation. In dialogue, people rarely pre-organize their thoughts. They don't necessarily use complete sentences or speak with proper grammar. People do not talk in prose. And because people do not talk in prose, scriptwriters do not write dialogue in prose. We do not stay bound to the traditional rules of composition. We reappropriate grammar. We create vocabulary. We employ rogue punctuation marks such as the ellipsis and the em dash. Your fourth grade teacher would be horrified, but your actors and your audience will thank you for it.

A few tips on dialogue punctuation:

- An ellipsis (...) suggests that a character's thought trails off.
- An em dash (–) suggests that a character stops a thought short, interrupts himself, or is interrupted by someone else.
- Periods create a pause or complete a thought. They work sort of like the word "stop" in a telegram. Forget what you learned in school. In dialogue, you don't need a complete sentence in order to use the period.

Here's an example:

```
                    MARK
          So. Right. There's this
          girl — she's not the type I
```

```
usually go out with. I usu-
ally go out with someone…
skinnier. More fit, you
know? But this girl — she's
fat. I mean FAT. And the
thing is, I think it's hot.
Yeah. Smokin'.
```

LESSON 1: SCRIPT ANALYSIS EXERCISE   ●

NOTE: In this exercise, beginning and intermediate writers should analyze published work by established writers. See the Appendix for a list of suggestions. Advanced writers have the option of bringing in their own work for analysis.

Have each member of the group bring in one page of dialogue from a play or screenplay. It's helpful to include a broad range of authors, genres, and writing styles.

For Discussion:

Review each page of dialogue with the group.
1. Describe the speaking style of each character.
2. How did the phrasing and punctuation of the dialogue contribute to your sense of each character's voice?
3. How does the style and rhythm of the dialogue contribute to the overall tone of the scene?

Is this a comic scene? A romantic scene? A melodramatic scene? What in the rhythm of the dialogue contributes to this impression?

4. Do you notice a difference in the style of dialogue from author to author? Compare and contrast your impressions.

▲ LESSON 1: BEGINNER EXERCISE

For this exercise, you will need a portable audio recorder. Interview two to three different people and ask them the same question. The question should be open-ended: one that can't be answered with a simple yes or no. (See below for a list of examples.) When selecting your interview subjects, try to find people as different from each other as possible: different ages, genders, socioeconomic backgrounds, nationalities, etc. It doesn't matter if your subjects know or remember all the details that the question asks – the point is to get them talking and to get them to answer the question as fully as possible in their own voice. Try to speak as little as possible while they answer.

Record each interview with an audio recorder. Then type up the interview word for word. As you type, try to capture the rhythm of the subject's speech in your punctuation.

Some suggestions for interview questions:

• What is your earliest memory?

- Describe the job of president of the United States.
- Tell me what happened in the most recent episode of your favorite television show.
- How did God create the world?
- Describe a dream that you had recently.

For Discussion:

1. Look over your transcriptions. Does anything surprise you? How does the transcription of the dialogue differ from traditional prose?

2. Have someone in the group (preferably someone with an acting background) read your transcription out loud. After the group member has read the transcription, play the original audio recording. In what ways did the reader sound different than the original speaker? Were there differences in the rhythm of the speech? Were there differences in emphasis or tone? If so, was there something in the way that the speech was transcribed onto the page that caused this difference?

3. What verbal habits or tics do you notice in the speaker's pattern of speech? For example: Is this a person who uses a particular phrase over and over? Is this a person who speaks in clipped, precise sentences? Is this a person who rambles

from topic to topic without ever completing a thought? Is this a person who can never come up with the word he's looking for?

4. What tones do you hear in the speaker's dialogue? Has the question provoked an emotional response such as anger, passion, or enthusiasm? How does the speaker seem to feel about what he is saying?

5. Have members of the group try to describe the speaker based on what they hear in the interview. What do you imagine that this person is like? Where do you think he lives? Where does he work? Who are his friends? What does he do in his free time?

■ **LESSON 1: INTERMEDIATE AND ADVANCED EXERCISE**

The following three paragraphs are from *Life on the Mississippi* by Mark Twain. The book is a memoir of his years working as a steamboat pilot on the Mississippi River. In this excerpt, Twain reflects on how his growing expertise of the river eventually killed his romance with it.

> Now when I had mastered the language of this water and had come to know every trifling feature that bordered the great river as familiarly as I knew the letters of the alphabet, I had made a valuable acquisition. But

I had lost something, too. I had lost something which could never be restored to me while I lived. All the grace, the beauty, the poetry had gone out of the majestic river! I still keep in mind a certain wonderful sunset which I witnessed when steamboating was new to me. . . . I stood like one bewitched. I drank it in, in a speechless rapture. The world was new to me, and I had never seen anything like this at home.

But as I have said, a day came when I began to cease from noting the glories and the charms which the moon and the sun and the twilight wrought upon the river's face… Then, if that sunset scene had been repeated, I should have looked upon it without rapture, and should have commented upon it, inwardly, after this fashion: This sun means that we are going to have wind tomorrow; that floating log means that the river is rising, small thanks to it; that slanting mark on the water refers to a bluff reef which is going to kill somebody's steamboat one of these nights, if it keeps on stretching out like that…

No, the romance and the beauty were all gone from the river. All the value any feature of it had for me now was the amount of

usefulness it could furnish toward compass-
ing the safe piloting of a steamboat. Since
those days, I have pitied doctors from my
heart. What does the lovely flush in a beauty's cheek mean to a doctor but a "break"
that ripples above some deadly disease. Are
not all her visible charms sown thick with
what are to him the signs and symbols of
hidden decay? Does he ever see her beauty
at all, or doesn't he simply view her profes-
sionally, and comment upon her unwhole-
some condition all to himself? And doesn't
he sometimes wonder whether he has gained
most or lost most by learning his trade?

The prose is beautifully written. But imagine if Twain
did not have the luxury of sitting down at a typewriter
and carefully composing his thoughts over several drafts.
Imagine instead that Twain told this story out loud, in
the moment, to someone standing in the room with
him. Rewrite this excerpt as that monologue.

For Discussion:

Have someone in the group read the original essay out
loud and then read her monologue version of it.

1. How did the monologue version differ from the
   prose version?
2. After all the monologues have been read,

compare and contrast the choices made by the monologue authors. In what ways were all the monologues the same? What were the differences?

3. Have each writer discuss the process of adapting the essay. What was the thought process that went into the choices by the writer? In what ways did the writer decide to stay faithful to the original text? In what ways did the writer feel free to diverge from the original text? How and why did the writer make those decisions?

4. Were there any aspects of the original piece that were particularly difficult to capture in monologue form? If so, why?

LESSON 1: SOLO EXERCISE ✚

Pick an excerpt from any piece of prose (e.g., an essay, newspaper article, or novel). Rewrite that excerpt as a monologue. The challenge is to stay as faithful as possible to the original tone, style, and content of the piece, but to re-create it as something spoken instead of read.

Now, rewrite that monologue. In the rewrite, keep the words of the monologue exactly the same, but change the punctuation. How much can you alter the tone and meaning of the monologue simply by changing the punctuation?

As an ongoing workout, experiment with different

source material. What kinds of prose are easy to adapt into monologues? What kinds are not? As you get better at adapting, challenge yourself by picking difficult selections.

TOMMY: What do you mean, I'm funny?... You mean the way I talk? What?... Funny how? I mean, what's funny about it?
—*Goodfellas* (1990)

LESSON TWO:
Imitating a Voice

Who are the voices in your head? Who are the people with speech so familiar to you that you can hear them talking when you close your eyes? In your life, who talks so distinctively and with such clarity of personality that you could imitate his rants, raves, sputterings, mumblings, or musings on any topic? Is it your crazy Aunt Tillie? Is it your rambling college professor? Is it your overly earnest ex-boyfriend?

You don't have to limit yourself to people you know personally. Consider the familiar and distinctive speech patterns of actors such as Jack Nicholson or television characters such as Tony Soprano or Homer Simpson. Consider other public figures. I've listened to the same local radio station for the past fifteen years. The patter of the morning DJ is as familiar to me as my morning shower.

Often, art students are given the assignment to copy an existing painting. The act of imitating another piece of art forces the artist to go beyond her typical choices and expand her repertoire. She must learn to use the heavy brush strokes of Van Gogh or the tiny meticulous dabs of Seurat. She will experiment with Rothko's layers of colors or Picasso's disjointed perspectives. Each of these exercises expands her skill set – a skill set that she can draw on in her future work.

By listening to the voices around us, and then attempting to imitate them on the page, we writers get a similar benefit. By tuning in to other people's distinctive patterns of speech, we hone our own ear for dialogue. By recreating those patterns on the page, we force ourselves to understand the nuances of those voices and we stretch our dialogue-writing technique into new territory.

● **LESSON 2: SCRIPT ANALYSIS EXERCISE**

NOTE: In this exercise, beginning and intermediate writers should analyze published work by established writers. See the Appendix for a list of suggestions. Advanced writers have the option of bringing in their own work for analysis.

Have the entire group see the same play, watch the same film, or read the same script. (See the Appendix for a list of suggestions.)

For Discussion:

1. Describe the speaking style for each character.

2. How did those styles differ from each other? How were they the same?

3. Which characters had the most memorable or unique voices? What made the voices memorable or unique?

4. Imagine you were writing an original scene for each character. As a writer, what would you do in the dialogue to capture each character's voice?

LESSON 2: BEGINNER EXERCISE ▲

1. By yourself or with a group, come up with a list of famous voices. They might be actors, public figures, or famous characters from television, stage, or film. Whoever they are, they should a) be well known; and b) have done an extensive amount of speaking. In other words, it's not enough for the person to be famous. He should also have a famous voice. Here are a few examples from one of my lists:
   - Kramer (from *Seinfeld*)
   - Bill O'Reilly
   - Tony Soprano
   - Barack Obama
   - Lisa Simpson (from *The Simpsons*)
   - Blanche DuBois

2. Each writer draws a name from the list of famous voices. The assignment is to write a monologue

in which that character speaks on the following topic:

> Describe your favorite color to someone who has been blind since birth.

3. As you write the monologue, you must follow these rules:
   - The goal is to imitate the voice as accurately and realistically as possible. Make sure that you avoid parody.
   - In the monologue, avoid names or references that could instantly identify the character. For example, if you are writing a monologue for Lisa Simpson, it is cheating to include a line like "That's what I told my brother, Bart," or "Here we are in Springfield."

For Discussion:

1. Read each monologue aloud to the group. Evaluate the personality of the voice. How would you describe this character? What in the dialogue influences your perception?
2. Have the group look at the character list and try to guess who the speaker is.
3. Survey the people who guessed correctly. What was it about the monologue that made them able to identify the character?

4. Survey the people who guessed incorrectly. What was it about the monologue that threw them off and left them unable to identify the character?

5. Were there any sections of the monologue where the writer cheated? Did he use any specific names or references that immediately gave away the identity of the speaker?

6. Have each writer discuss how he approached the monologue. What specific vocal patterns did he notice in the character's speech and try to recreate in the monologue? What was the most challenging aspect of writing the monologue? In approaching the challenging parts, what did the writer do to overcome those challenges? What insights about dialogue writing can be gleaned from that approach?

LESSON 2: INTERMEDIATE AND ADVANCED EXERCISE

1. For this exercise, you will need to select a person whose voice is unfamiliar to you. This might be a distant acquaintance or it might be a well-documented but still obscure public figure. Whoever it is, the person should be real (not fictional). Immerse yourself in that person's voice for a week. If you know the person, interview

her in detail and ask her about her life. Spend as much time as possible with her in different social settings. If the person is a public figure, spend a week listening to her speeches, public interviews, or broadcasts. Read material that will give you background information on her life (interviews, biographies, memoirs, etc).

2. After spending the week becoming familiar with the new subject, write a monologue capturing that person's voice. The monologue can be on any subject you wish, but it must obey the following rules:
   - The monologue must be completely original. Do not simply cobble together existing statements by the subject.
   - The monologue must be set in a particular time and place and it must be spoken to a particular person or people. In stage directions before the monologue, describe where the subject is when she speaks. Describe exactly whom she is speaking to.

For Discussion:

Each author should read his monologue out loud to the group. *Do not* read the stage directions out loud, only the monologue.

1. Upon hearing the monologue, what are the group's impressions of the speaker? How would the group describe her?
2. What verbal habits or tics do you notice in the speaker?
3. What is the subject of the monologue? What emotional overtones does it convey?
4. Where and when does the monologue take place? Who is the subject speaking to? What other context can you glean from the monologue?
5. Why is the speaker saying this monologue? What motivates her to speak these words?
6. Ask the author: How do the group's impressions differ (if at all) from your intent? Did the group miss out on anything that you intended to convey? Did the group read anything in to the monologue that surprised you?
7. If there are different interpretations of the monologue, try to identify the elements of the monologue that led to those different interpretations.

After hearing all the monologues out loud, discuss the following:

1. When your group answered the questions above, there may have been conflicting opinions over the interpretation of some monologues. There

may have been distance between what the author wrote and what the audience inferred. When is it acceptable for different audience members to have different interpretations of something that a character says? When is it acceptable for the audience to infer something that the author did not intend? When is it not acceptable?

2. Which monologues gave you the most sense of context? Which ones gave you the clearest sense of who the speaker was, where he was located, whom he was speaking to, why he was speaking, etc.? What was it about those monologues that allowed you to make such clear inferences?

✛ LESSON 2: SOLO EXERCISE

This exercise requires a bit of eavesdropping. When you are out in public, listen in on a nearby conversation. Note the location, tone, and subject matter of the conversation. Zero in on one of the conversation participants. Focus on that person. Listen for the particular personality of that person's voice. Jot down three quotes from him as he speaks.

Take the three quotes and weave them into an original monologue that captures the conversation participant's voice. The monologue can be on the same subject as the overheard conversation, or it can be on a completely different subject.

LESSON THREE:
Creating an Original Voice

The Jazz Singer

I am reading a review of a red wine:

> This blend of Merlot and Cabernet Frac...
> tastes of ripe black fruits (blackberry, black
> currant, boysenberry), with hints of vanilla,
> cocoa, and brown spices from the oak
> treatment.

The most interesting voices, like the most interesting wines, contain a mix of flavors. Good writers weave multiple facets into a character's speech. Each voice is a blend of personality traits and social habits. There are overtones and undertones; there are bold statements and subtle hints. All of these come together to create a multifaceted flavor.

The easiest way to come up with an original character voice is to be one of those writers who has such a good ear for dialogue and such a strong sense of character that the voices simply start talking in your head. You can hear them even before you start writing.

However, if you're one of us mere mortals, you are going to have to rely on the second easiest method of coming up with an original character voice. You are going to have to identify the particular mix of personality traits and social habits that define your character. Then you are going to have to create the sound of that mix in speech. How does a nervous person talk? How does a dictatorial person talk? How does a person who is *both* nervous and dictatorial talk?

Always remember that the most interesting voices and the best dialogue writing come with a blend of flavors. Characters who speak with only one tone and in only one dimension are flat, predictable, and stereotypical. The most powerful technique for adding interest to a character's voice is to add multiple dimensions to that voice.

LESSON 3: **SCRIPT ANALYSIS EXERCISE** ●

NOTE: In this exercise, beginning and intermediate writers should analyze published work by established authors. See the Appendix for a list of suggestions. Advanced writers have the option of bringing in their own work for analysis.

Have each writer bring in a two- to three-page dialogue scene from a play or screenplay. Make sure that everyone has the opportunity to read the scenes to themselves (not out loud) before the beginning of the discussion.

For Discussion:

1. What tones do you hear in each character's voice?
2. What do those tones tell you about each character in this scene?
3. Is the group in any disagreement about the tones? (For example, does one reader feel that a character is being sarcastic while another feels that a character is being sincere?) If so, what in the script has led to these different interpretations?
4. What lines, in particular, bring out the strongest or clearest tones?
5. What lines, in particular, seem to have multiple tones or dimensions?

6. Does the balance of tones in each character's voice ever shift? If so, when? Why?

7. Do any tones seem to be missing? For example, is there some bit of subtext or tension going on in the scene that does not seem to manifest itself in the dialogue?

▲ LESSON 3: BEGINNER EXERCISE

This is a list of tones you might hear in a character's voice. Feel free to add to the list.

abrasive	detail-oriented	laid-back
alert	domineering	lonely
anxious	eager	meek
arrogant	erratic	morose
bewildered	excitable	naive
bitter	exuberant	nervous
bored	fanatical	ominous
bright	fearful	opinionated
calm	fearless	optimistic
cheerful	flippant	paranoid
clumsy	frank	pessimistic
commanding	furtive	precise
creepy	gentle	proud
cultured	grouchy	reckless
decorous	guilty	reflective
defiant	hesitant	romantic
deranged	jittery	sarcastic

sensitive	taciturn	willful
short-tempered	vague	wry
shrewd	verbose	zany
squeamish	vulgar	
sullen	weary	

1. Select one adjective from the list (or draw it out of a hat). Write a monologue with that tone (and only that tone) underlying it.
2. Select another adjective from the list (or draw it out of a hat). Rewrite the previous monologue so that both tones blend into it.
3. In writing the monologues, there is only one rule. The character is never allowed to explicitly tell us the underlying tone. It's cheating to write "I feel sullen," or "I am detail-oriented."

For Discussion:

1. Read the first monologue aloud to the group. Have the group guess which adjective was the underlying tone for the speech.
2. Why? What is it about the monologue that leads members of the group to select that adjective?
3. Does the writer ever cheat? Is there any point in the monologue where you feel the writer has explicitly told the audience what the underlying tone is supposed to be? If so, where? Could you cut that section out of the monologue and still

have the monologue communicate the selected tone?

4. Have the writer reveal which tone word was behind the monologue. If the tone that the writer chose is different than the tone that the group believed it to be, discuss the difference in meaning between the two words. What are the variations in the shades of meaning? How do you recognize that subtle difference in speech?

5. Read the second monologue out loud to the group. Have the group guess which adjective was the second underlying tone for the speech.

6. How did the addition of the second tone change the monologue?

7. After everyone has presented their assignments, discuss which tone combinations made for the most interesting voices. Why were those combinations more effective?

■ **LESSON 3: INTERMEDIATE AND ADVANCED EXERCISE**

Look at the list of words in the Beginner Exercise. It is a list of tones you might hear in a character's voice. Feel free to add to the list.

Select four words from the list (or draw them out of a hat). Write a monologue that blends all four tones together into one character's voice.

For Discussion:

1. Read the monologue out loud to the group. Have the group guess which adjectives supplied the underlying tones to the speech.
2. Why? What is it about the monologue that leads members of the group to select those adjectives?
3. Have the writer reveal which adjectives were behind the monologue. If the words that the writer chose were different than the words that the group selected, try to identify which aspects of the monologue led to the differing opinions.
4. Discuss the balance of the tones in the monologue. Were some tones more dominant than others? What does the relative weight of all of the tones tell you about the character?
5. For the writer: Discuss how the four adjectives helped or hindered your monologue writing process. What choices did the adjectives force you to make? What limitations did they impose? In what ways was that helpful? In what ways was that frustrating?

LESSON 3: SOLO EXERCISE ✛

There are distinctive voices all around you. They exist in the people you know, in the characters you see on screen or on stage, in the magazines or blogs that you read, and in the public figures you hear every day.

1. Seek out four distinctive voices in the social, political and cultural environment. Try to vary your sources. (Don't pick four voices exclusively from television, for example. Don't exclusively pick four sarcastic people.) Here's a sample list of voices:
   - My husband (a person I know)
   - *Maxim* (a magazine)
   - Jerry Lundergaard (William H. Macy's character from the movie *Fargo*)
   - Oprah Winfrey (a talk show host)

2. Once you have your list, write at least three adjectives that describe the tones underlying that voice. It's okay if your judgment is subjective. Here's a sample list:
   - My husband (a person I know): intellectually driven; articulate; sarcastic
   - *Maxim* (a magazine): cocky; adolescent; hipster
   - Jerry Lundergaard (William H. Macy's character from the movie *Fargo*): dim-witted; desperate; chip on his shoulder
   - Oprah Winfrey (a talk show host): earnest; matronly; charismatic

3. Now, remove the names and just look at the list of adjectives. Again, here is the sample:

adolescent

articulate

charismatic

chip on shoulder

cocky

desperate

dim-witted

earnest

hipster

intellectually driven

matronly

sarcastic

4. Randomly select three adjectives from your list and write an original monologue that blends those tones together into an original voice.

5. Repeat this exercise regularly as an ongoing writer's workout. Create a permanent file for each new voice that you develop. In the future, when you are developing characters for scenes and full-length scripts, you can refer back to these files for ideas and inspiration.

DIALOGUE: HOW PEOPLE TALK TO EACH OTHER

LESSON FOUR:
Status

Let's begin with a fact that underlies all human interaction. Human beings are animals – literally. With our advanced brains, our sophisticated language skills, and our stunning fashion sense, it's easy to forget that – deep down – we still carry instincts from our mammalian ancestors.

In his book, *Impro*, Keith Johnstone argues that humans, like animals, take on status roles in their interactions with one other. These status roles are more flexible and more complicated than the behaviors that define the status of pack animals, but at a fundamental level they can be broken down into two similar categories:

- Low status: characterized by subordination or deference to others
- High status: characterized by superiority, primacy, or dominance over others

If you listen, you can hear these status roles reflected in the way people talk:

VERY LOW STATUS: If you're not using it, could you please pass that pen?

LOW STATUS: Please pass the pen.

HIGH STATUS: Give me the pen.

VERY HIGH STATUS: Pen. Now.

And:

VERY LOW STATUS: How are you feeling? Are you thirsty? Should I get you a drink?

LOW STATUS: If you're thirsty, let me get you a drink.

HIGH STATUS: You look thirsty. I'm getting you a drink.

VERY HIGH STATUS: You're thirsty. Go get something to drink.

Status is an incredibly powerful tool in the writing of dialogue. It influences not only how people speak, but also how they interact with each other. It adjusts itself from line to line and moment to moment. Most important, there is something about status that is instinctive. You do not need to explain status interactions to an audience. High status and low status cues are hard wired into our brains. Millions of years of evolution have designed us to instantly recognize when someone is asserting dominance, when someone is challenging dominance, and when someone is being subordinate. These social cues allowed our animal ancestors to lay claim to food, recognize threats, and share in resources. As humans evolved, as we developed language, tools, civilization, and culture, this primal understanding has taken on many complicated layers. But the underlying forces of dominance and subordination, of primacy and deference, still influence our speech and behavior.

This entire section of the book will be devoted to status and the myriad ways that it plays out in human interaction and dialogue. For this lesson, let's just focus on crafting lines that reflect different status levels.

LESSON 4: SCRIPT ANALYSIS EXERCISE ●

Neil Simon's dialogue tends to have very clear and simple status interactions. Have the group review three different dialogue scenes from Neil Simon plays or screenplays. (See the Appendix for a list of suggestions.) Choose scenes that contain only two characters and are two to three pages in length.

Individually or as a group, go through each scene line by line. Identify the status role that the speaker is taking in each line. Make a note next to each line:

- VL = very low status
- L = low status
- H = high status
- VH = very high status

For Discussion:

1. Did you notice a trend for any of the characters? Which characters had a tendency to play high status? Which characters had a tendency to play low status?
2. Did characters ever break their status trend? If so, when? Why?
3. How did the characters' status tactics affect your impression of their personalities?
4. How did the characters' status interactions affect your understanding of their relationship?

▲ LESSON 4: BEGINNER EXERCISE

For each of the activities below, write a line or two of dialogue that reflects how the very low status, the low status, the high status, and the very high status player would accomplish this activity:

- Ordering a cup of coffee, with sugar, in a restaurant
- Asking someone out on a date
- Talking a cop out of a speeding ticket
- Asking someone to pay back a debt

For Discussion:

1. Randomly read the lines out loud to the group. Have the group guess which status role the speaker was taking.

2. What in the line made the group select that status role?

3. If the status role that the group guessed is different than the status role that the writer intended, discuss what it was in the writing that caused the discrepancy.

4. Compare and contrast the very low status lines with each other. How are they similar? How are they different?

5. Compare and contrast the low status lines with each other. How are they similar? How are they different?

6. Compare and contrast the high status lines with each other. How are they similar? How are they different?

7. Compare and contrast the very high status lines with each other. How are they similar? How are they different?

LESSON 4: INTERMEDIATE AND ADVANCED EXERCISE

Rather than just four levels of status (very low, low, high, and very high), imagine that there are ten. They exist on a spectrum from the very, very, very, very low to the very, very, very, very high.

Starting with the very, very, very, very low, write a line of dialogue in which a character asks someone out on a date. Rewrite the line nine more times. With each rewrite, raise the status of the speaker one notch along the spectrum. Your final line should have the speaker taking on a very, very, very, very high status role.

For Discussion:

1. In random order, read each writer's lines out loud to the group. Have the group try to place the lines on the status spectrum. Can the group organize the lines from one to ten?

2. If the group has trouble placing any of the lines on the spectrum, discuss what it is about the line that makes it difficult to place.

3. After placing all the lines, have a member of the group read them out loud in sequence.

4. Have the group member read them out loud again. This time, the group member should read the same sequence, but try to invert the status role of each line using his voice and manner. For example: Try to read the very, very, very, very high status line in a very, very, very, very low status way. Read the very low status line in a very high status way.

5. What tricks of voice and manner did the speaker use to try to shift the status of the line?

6. Were those tricks successful? Is it possible to

make a low status line read as high status simply by changing your tone or manner? Is it possible to make a high status line read as low status simply by changing your tone or manner?

7. What is the effect of hearing a low status line read in a high status way? What is the effect of hearing a high status line read in a low status way?

8. If it is possible for an actor to invert the status of a line using his voice and manner, then how might an actor or director evaluate a line to decide which status level is appropriate?

LESSON 4: **SOLO EXERCISE**   +

1. Write the numbers one through ten on slips of paper and put them in a hat. These numbers represent levels on a spectrum of status. Number one is very, very, very, very low status. Number ten is very, very, very, very high status. Number five is halfway between.

2. Select a character from one of your scripts, scenes, or exercises. Draw a number out of the hat. Write a line of dialogue in which your character takes on that status level.

3. Draw another number out of the hat. Rewrite the same line of dialogue to take on the new status level.

4. Repeat step 3 until you have drawn all the numbers out of the hat.

5. Repeat this exercise regularly as an ongoing writer's workout.

LESSON FIVE:
Give and Take

Keith Johnstone notes that status does not exist in a vacuum. An individual's status is always defined relative to the people around him. The low status player must always keep himself lower than the people around him. The high status player must always keep herself higher than the people around her. In human interaction and in human conversation, high status and low status aren't fixed marks; they are moving targets. This means that, as dialogue moves, every individual adjusts his status to move along with it.

How do characters do this? Consider the following line:

> PERSON A: I baked some chocolate chip cookies.

In response to this line, the low status person must place himself lower than the person who just spoke. He does this by either lowering his own status:

> LOW STATUS: God, I can't bake anything. My cookies are always a disaster.

41

Or raising the status of the other person:

> LOW STATUS: Mmmmmm. You know I
> am a slave to your chocolate chip cookies!

In response to the same line, the high status person must place herself higher than the person who just spoke. She does this by either raising her own status:

> HIGH STATUS: Cookies! I make mine
> with walnuts. People love them. I sold four-
> teen dozen at the school bake sale.

Or lowering the status of the other person:

> HIGH STATUS: Finally, you baked some-
> thing that you didn't burn!

Line by line, characters have the power to give and take status. When characters engage in this dance, when they adjust their status levels moment to moment, it brings the dialogue to life. It creates a dynamic backdrop for a scene. It puts the characters on a constantly shifting playing field. As a dialogue writer, you should practice this give and take between characters. Learn to pass status back and forth expertly and deftly.

● **LESSON 5: SCRIPT ANALYSIS EXERCISE**

Have the group attend the same play or watch the same film. (See the Appendix for a list of suggestions.) Get a copy of the script. Have each member of the group

review the script on his own and find an example of a
two-line exchange of dialogue in which:

1. A character attempts to lower his status beneath
   that of the person who just spoke.
2. A character attempts to raise another character's
   status.
3. A character attempts to raise his own status
   above that of the person who just spoke.
4. A character attempts to lower another character's status.

Print out the dialogue exchanges and share them
with the group.

For Discussion:

1. Read the dialogue exchanges randomly out
   loud to the class. Have the group try to guess
   which status goal above (1, 2, 3, or 4) the group
   member was trying to illustrate.
2. Was there any disagreement in the opinions? If
   so, what in the writing led to the disagreement?
3. After all the lines have been read, compare and
   contrast the tactics that different characters used
   to lower their status beneath that of the person
   who just spoke. How were they similar? How
   were they different?
4. After all the lines have been read, compare and
   contrast the tactics that different characters used

to raise another character's status. How were they similar? How were they different?

5. After all the lines have been read, compare and contrast the tactics that different characters used to raise their own status above the person who just spoke. How were they similar? How were they different?

6. After all the lines have been read, compare and contrast the tactics that different characters used to lower another character's status. How were they similar? How were they different?

▲ LESSON 5: BEGINNER EXERCISE

For each of the lines of dialogue below, write a response from:

1. A character attempting to lower his status beneath that of the speaker.
2. A character attempting to raise the speaker's status.
3. A character attempting to raise his status above that of the speaker.
4. A character attempting to lower the speaker's status.

Starting lines:
- It's cold outside.
- Could I borrow your car?

- My play is going to Broadway!
- I love your shoes.
- I'm sorry about the mess.

Write each exchange in dialogue form. Here's an example.

PERSON A: It's cold outside.

PERSON B (fluffing her fur coat): Not when you're wearing a mink.

When you've finished the exercise, you should have twenty different dialogue exchanges (four different responses to five different opening lines). Write each exchange out on an index card.

For Discussion:

1. Collect the index cards and put them in a hat. Draw an index card randomly. Have two group members act out the dialogue exchange on the card.
2. Identify the writer of the dialogue exchange. Have the group try to guess which status goal (1, 2, 3 or 4) the writer was trying to achieve.
3. Was there any discrepancy between what the group guessed and what the writer intended? If so, try to identify what in the writing led to this discrepancy.

4. After you've reviewed at least ten different dialogue exchanges, make a list of which lines created the biggest status gaps between the first speaker and the second. What was the effect or impression created by those large status gaps?
5. Make a list of which lines created the smallest status gaps between the first speaker and the second. What was the effect or impression created by those small status gaps?

■ LESSON 5: INTERMEDIATE AND ADVANCED EXERCISE

1. Pick one of the starting lines of dialogue below:
   - It's cold outside.
   - Could I borrow your car?
   - My play is going to Broadway!
   - I love your shoes.
   - I'm sorry about the mess.
2. In response to each starting line of dialogue, write ten different responses from *a low status person attempting to lower his status beneath that of the speaker.* Start by having the low status person place his status only slightly lower. With each rewrite of the line, expand the status gap. By the tenth rewrite of the line, the low status person should be placing himself ten times lower than the speaker.

3. In response to the same starting line of dialogue, write ten different responses from *a low status person attempting to raise the speaker's status.* Start by having the low status person raise the speaker's status only slightly higher. With each rewrite of the line, expand the status gap. By the tenth rewrite of the line, the low status person should be raising the speaker's status ten times higher than the speaker.

4. In response to the same starting line of dialogue, write ten different responses from *a high status person attempting to raise his status above that of the speaker.* Start by having the high status person raise his own status only slightly higher than the speaker. With each rewrite of the line, expand the status gap. By the tenth rewrite of the line, the high status person should be placing himself ten times higher than the speaker.

5. In response to the same starting line of dialogue, write ten different responses from *a high status person attempting to lower the speaker's status.* Start by having the high status person lower the speaker's status only slightly. With each rewrite of the line, expand the status gap. By the tenth rewrite of the line, the high status person should be lowering the speaker's status by a factor of ten.

For Discussion:

1. Have each writer read one of her sets of ten lines out loud. She should read these lines in random order.

2. Have the group guess which set of ten lines from the exercise assignment (2, 3, 4, or 5) the writer was attempting to create.

3. Have the group organize the lines along a spectrum spanning the smallest status gap to the largest status gap.

4. What is the difference between large status gaps and small status gaps? Do they have a different effect on the audience? Do they give you different impressions of a character?

✚ LESSON 5: SOLO EXERCISE

1. Write the numbers one through ten on slips of paper and put them in a hat. In this drill, the numbers will represent increments of status.

2. Write an opening line of dialogue for Character A.

3. Pick *one* of the following four options for the responding character (Character B):

   • The low status person attempting to lower his status beneath that of the speaker.

   • The low status person attempting to raise the speaker's status.

- The high status person attempting to raise his status above that of the speaker.
- The high status person attempting to lower the speaker's status.

4. Draw a number out of the hat. This number is the size of the status increment that Character B should try to achieve. For example, if you draw a number ten, Character B should attempt to raise or lower his status by a very, very, very, very large amount. If you draw a number one, Character B will raise or lower his status by only a miniscule amount.

5. Draw another number out of the hat. Rewrite the first line to reflect this new status gap.

6. Repeat step 5 until you have used all the numbers.

7. Arrange all the lines on a spectrum from one to ten. Are there any gaps? Between existing lines, could you add new lines with shades of status difference? If so, write them.

8. Could you add more? Could you write status gaps in increments of eleven, twelve, thirteen, fourteen, and fifteen? If so, write them.

9. Repeat this exercise regularly as an ongoing writer's workout.

LESSON SIX:
Building Dialogue

Gone with the Wind

Think about the people around you. Who are the high status players? Who are the people who, in every line of every conversation, try to take positions of superiority and prominence? Who are the low status players? Who are the people who, in every line of every conversation, try to take positions of subordination and deference?

In dialogue, status isn't just a role, it's an agenda. Many people are able to adjust that agenda to suit the needs of the moment. (We'll talk about those people in later chapters.) For now, we're going to focus on inflexible status players. These are people who work to maintain their preferred status role throughout an entire conversation. No matter how appropriate or inappropriate it is, inflexible low status players will always keep themselves low. They will quickly spiral down to absurd depths to maintain the lower status role. Inflexible high status players will always keep themselves high. They will quickly escalate their conversation to absurd heights to maintain the higher status role.

Let's experiment with how this plays out in a conversation.

● **LESSON 6: SCRIPT ANALYSIS EXERCISE**

In this exercise, the group will go on a scavenger hunt. Randomly assign each member one of the following:

- A scene between two relentlessly high status players
- A scene between two relentlessly low status players
- A scene between a relentlessly high status player and a relentlessly low status player

Once each member has her assignment, she must find a scene from an existing play or screenplay that matches the description she was given. (She can use the Appendix for suggestions or she can find material on her own.) She should look for a one- to three-page, one- to three-minute dialogue scene between only two people. She can either bring in pages from the script or clips from the film or TV show.

For Discussion:

Have each member of the group present the script pages or video clips.

1. Have the group guess the status relationship between the two characters.
2. Did the group guess correctly? If so, what in the script made the status relationship clear? If not, what in the script made the status relationship confusing?
3. Look at all the scenes between two relentlessly high status players. What do they all have in common? How do they differ?
4. Look at all the scenes between the two relentlessly low status players. What do they all have in common? How do they differ?
5. Look at all the scenes between the relentlessly high status players and the relentlessly low status players. What do they all have in common? How do they differ?

▲ LESSON 6: BEGINNER EXERCISE

1. Write a two- or three-page dialogue between two characters. In the dialogue, the characters should discuss one of the following topics:
   - The weather
   - A famous book, movie, or TV show
   - A sports team or a particular sporting event
2. Before you start writing, randomly assign each character one of the status preferences below:
   - Very low status
   - Low status
   - High status
   - Very high status
3. As you write the dialogue, make sure each character does everything he can to maintain his preferred status level throughout the conversation. A high status person will, in every line, try to place his status slightly higher than the person who just spoke. A very high status person will, in every line, try to place his status much higher than the person who just spoke. A low status person will always go slightly lower than the person who just spoke; a very low status person will always go much lower.

For Discussion:

Read the dialogues aloud to the group.

1. Have the group guess which status role each character was playing.

2. Was there any point at which a character broke out of her preferred role? For example, if the character was assigned high status, did she ever break into low status? Did she ever jump into very high status? If so, when did it happen? Why did it happen? What drove the character to break out of her preferred status role?

3. Identify the techniques that each character used to maintain her status role. When did she raise or lower her own status? When did she raise or lower the other person's status?

4. Discuss the status gaps between the characters in the dialogues. Which status gaps created the most realistic dialogue? Which status gaps created the least realistic dialogue? Which status gaps made the characters seem reasonable? Which status gaps made the characters seem crazy, neurotic, or funny?

LESSON 6: INTERMEDIATE AND ADVANCED EXERCISE

In this exercise, you will write a three- to five-page dialogue between three characters.

1. In the dialogue, the characters should discuss one of the following topics:
   - The weather
   - A famous book, movie, or TV show
   - A sports team or a particular sporting event
2. Before you begin, draw the following diagram:

3. Now, randomly assign each character a preferred status role in relation to each of the other characters. It will look something like this:

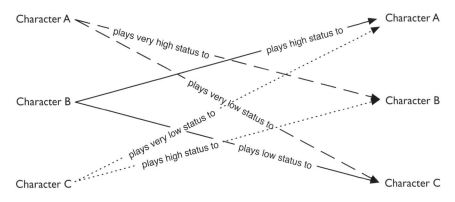

4. Write the scene. Have each character maintain, throughout the dialogue, his preferred status role in relation to each of the other characters. In the above example, Character A will, throughout the conversation, try to keep himself very high status relative to Character B. At the same time, Character A will, throughout the conversation, try to keep himself very low status relative to Character C.

For Discussion:

Read the dialogues out loud.

1. After listening to a dialogue, have the group try to re-create the starting diagram. What status role did each character try to take on with each of the other characters?

2. Was there any point at which a character broke out of her preferred role in relation to another character? For example, if the character was assigned high status, did she ever break into low status? Did she ever jump into very high status? If so, when did it happen? Why did it happen? What drove the character to break out of her preferred status role?

3. How did the prescribed status roles guide the writer in creating the dialogue?

4. What interesting or surprising moments came about as a result of the prescribed status roles?

5. How did the prescribed status roles affect the dynamic of the dialogue?

✛ LESSON 6: SOLO EXERCISE

1. Brainstorm a list of at least three topics that have come up in your life in the last week. For example, here's my list:
   • Pregnancy
   • The presidential election
   • Halloween

2. For each item on the list, brainstorm at least three specific issues that have come up around the topics. Here's my example:
   • Pregnancy
     ▪ What to name the baby
     ▪ Heartburn
     ▪ Buying maternity clothes
   • The presidential election
     ▪ Not getting work done because I am reading the latest political polls
     ▪ Early voting
     ▪ Trying to compose a letter on behalf of my candidate
   • Halloween
     ▪ Going a little overkill on the Halloween decorations

- ■ Deciding what candy to buy
- ■ Scheduling trick-or-treating

3. Now, pick one of the specific issues from your list. Write a two-person dialogue in which two fictional characters in a fictional setting deal with that same issue. Before you start writing, randomly assign each character one of the status preferences below

   - very low status
   - low status
   - high status
   - very high status

   As you write the dialogue, make sure each character does everything he can to maintain his preferred status level throughout the conversation.

4. Repeat this exercise regularly as an ongoing writer's workout.

> BENJAMIN: Mrs. Robinson, you're trying to seduce me. Aren't you?
> —*The Graduate* (1967)

LESSON SEVEN:
Dialogue on Shifting Sands

The Graduate

It's not only people who try to give and take status. An environment can give and take status just as effectively as an individual. Think about architecture. What buildings and environments are clearly designed to make you feel small, as if you are in the presence of something larger and more important than yourself? St. Peter's Basilica... the Capitol Building in Washington, DC... a CEO's plush executive office... these are just a few that leap to my mind. Now, what buildings and environments are clearly designed to make you feel grand, as if you are important and significant? The interior of a stretch limousine... your table at a fancy restaurant... the inside of a luxury spa.

Social environments also attempt to manipulate status. Look at any human community: the United Nations, the music industry, a garden club, or even your friends gathered in a coffee shop. You will see that one of the things that each community does is to attempt to define status and status roles. That decision is a collective one based on the group's values and needs. A man who shows off his knowledge of how to grow a prizewinning orchid might be admired by a garden club, but teased in a sports bar. An oil company executive might be the honorary guest at a business dinner, but the subject of protests by an environmentalist group. A suicide bomber is considered a terrorist by one group of people, but a martyr by another.

Even within a particular community, status roles are not immutable. Events can trigger a change in the way a group assigns status. Imagine a gathering of people attending a political fund-raiser. The guest of honor is a candidate for president. He's giving a speech. That candidate is in a very high status position. Everyone is there to listen to him (and perhaps to give him money). Now imagine that one of the guests collapses with chest pain. The candidate has no idea what to do. The guests ask around for a doctor. The doctor in the room steps forward. Now the doctor has the highest status in the room. Everyone expects the doctor to take control of the situation. Until the crisis is over, the room will defer to the doctor's authority. The high status position has switched from the candidate to the doctor as a result of the change of circumstance in the room.

On a smaller scale, this happens even as people jump from topic to topic in conversation. My husband, Jeremy, is a computer programmer who knows nothing about sports. When talking sports, our friends will tease him about his cluelessness (lowering his status); however, if the topic switches to the best way to back up a hard drive, these same people will start asking for Jeremy's opinion (raising his status).

Every day, human beings move from place to place, from community to community, and from moment to moment. This ever-changing landscape demands status deftness. An individual might have an innate preference for playing high status or low status, but everyone must – to some degree – do both. The diversity of human society demands it. From place to place, from community to community, and from moment to moment, we jockey for status position on a constantly shifting playing field.

LESSON 7: SCRIPT ANALYSIS EXERCISE ●

Select a dialogue scene from a film or television show. (See the Appendix for a list of suggestions.) The scene should contain no more than three people.

For Discussion:

Play the scene with the sound on mute. Without hearing any dialogue, try to answer the following questions:

- Which characters are playing high status and which characters are playing low status? Without the dialogue, how can you tell?
- Do the status roles shift in the scene? If so, when? Without the dialogue, how could you tell that the status roles shifted?

Replay the scene with the volume on.

- How does the dialogue reveal the status roles?
- How do the dialogue shifts match up with the shifts in status?
- Does something happen in the scene to trigger the status shift? If so, what?
- Does the dialogue reflect the shifts in status? If so, how?

▲ **LESSON 7: BEGINNER EXERCISE**

In this exercise, you will write a two- to three-page dialogue between two characters.

1. Randomly assign each character one of the following status roles:
   - very low status
   - low status
   - high status
   - very high status

DIALOGUE ON SHIFTING SANDS

2. For the first half of the dialogue, each character must maintain his preferred status role. Halfway through the dialogue, find a way to make the characters switch to new status roles. Maintain those new roles through to the end.

For Discussion:

Read the dialogues out loud to the group.

1. What was each character's preferred status role in the first half of the dialogue? Did he consistently maintain that role throughout the first half?

2. What was each character's preferred status role in the second half of the dialogue? Did he consistently maintain that role throughout the second half?

3. What caused the characters to switch to new roles?

4. What was the effect of having the characters switch to new status roles? What new information did it give you about the characters, their situation, and their relationship?

5. How did the switching of the status roles affect the tone of the dialogue? Did big status shifts have a different effect on tone than small status shifts?

■ LESSON 7: INTERMEDIATE AND ADVANCED EXERCISE

In this exercise, you will write a three- to five-page dialogue between three characters.

    1. Before you begin, draw the following diagram:

Character A   Character A

Character B   Character B

Character C   Character C

    2. Now, randomly assign each character a preferred status role in relation to each of the other characters. It will look something like this:

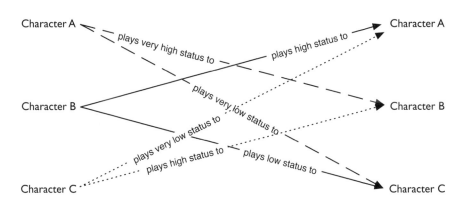

3. Now, draw a second diagram with a completely
   different set of status relationships between the
   characters. For example:

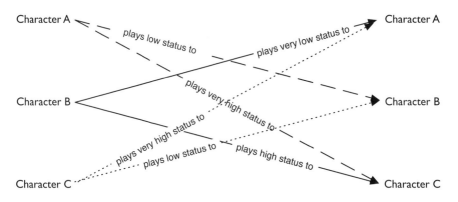

4. Write the dialogue. In the first half of the scene,
   each character must maintain the status roles as
   described in the first diagram. Halfway through
   the dialogue, find a reason for the characters to
   switch to the status roles in the second diagram.
   Have them maintain those roles through to the
   end.

For Discussion:

Read the dialogues out loud to the group.

1. After listening to a dialogue, have the group try
   to re-create the starting diagram and the ending
   diagram.

2. In the first half of the dialogue, did each character consistently maintain his preferred status

role in relation to each of the other characters? If there was a break, when did it happen? Why did it happen?

3. In the second half of the dialogue, did each character consistently maintain his new preferred status role in relation to each of the other characters? If there was a break, when did it happen? Why did it happen?

4. In the scene, what caused the characters to switch to new status roles?

5. What was the effect of having the characters switch status roles? What new information did it give you about the characters, their situation, and their relationship?

6. How did the switching of the status roles affect the tone of the dialogue? Did big status shifts have a different effect on tone than small status shifts?

✚ **LESSON 7: SOLO EXERCISE**

You will write a three- to five-page scene between two characters: Character A and Character B.

1. Before you begin, write numbers one through ten out on slips of paper and put them in a hat. These numbers represent levels on a spectrum of status. Number one is very, very, very, very

low status. Number ten is very, very, very, very high status. Number five is halfway between.

2. Draw three numbers from the hat. Character A must start the scene with the status level of the first number. At some point in the scene, he must flip his status to the second number. By the end of the scene, he must change his status to the third number.

3. Write the scene.

4. Repeat this exercise regularly as an ongoing writer's workout.

NOTE: For an Advanced Solo Exercise, draw three numbers for both Character A *and* Character B. Write the scene so that both characters go through all three of their status levels by the end of the scene.

LESSON EIGHT:
Strengths and Weaknesses

Managing status relationships is a complicated dance. It is an ever-evolving two-part calculation. It involves: 1) knowing when to raise or lower your status; and 2) knowing how to do it.

Knowing When to Raise and Lower Your Status

Imagine that you are the CEO of a company. What status role should you take on?

1. Should you be a relentlessly high status CEO? This CEO is domineering, micromanaging, and never defers to his employees on anything.

2. Should you be a relentlessly low status CEO? This CEO is submissive, passive, and never questions or challenges his employees on anything.

3. Should you be a CEO who is able to adjust his status? This CEO is able to be decisive and assert his authority when necessary. However, he also solicits input from his employees and relies on them for their advice and expertise.

TALK THE TALK ■ PENNISTON

We live in a culture that places value on high status, but as you can see, high status is not always the best status. The most effective people are able to raise or lower their status to match the needs of the moment. Two fundamentals that will define your character are how flexible he is in taking on different status roles in different circumstances, and how clever he is in making those choices.

Knowing How to Raise or Lower Your Status

Knowing when to raise or lower your status is only half the battle. You must also successfully accomplish this shift. Ultimately, you might play high status, but you're only in a high status position if other people treat you as high status.

Have you ever watched a child try to order an adult around, only to have the adult laugh at that child for being cute? Do you remember the nerdy, insecure kid in high school who tried to act cool? Do you remember any teachers, camp counselors, or bosses who tried to exert their authority, but no one listened to them? These are examples of people who are trying to play high status, but who are not effective at it. Despite their best efforts, they were not able to take the high status ground.

On the other hand, you have probably seen the opposite: people who attempt to lower their status, but fail. Have you ever had someone try to compliment you, only to have it feel like an insult? Have you ever seen an adult try to talk baby talk to a child, only to have the child cower and cry?

Human society demands status deftness, but individuals are not always up to the task. Every person has status strengths and weaknesses. In a perfect world, we would all expertly raise or lower our status to perfectly suit the needs of the moment. But this is not a perfect world, and drama is never about a perfect world. Characters inevitably stumble in the status dance. They play high status when they ought to play low. They try to take low status, but end up lifted high. These mistakes are the stuff of great drama, great comedy, and great dialogue.

Writing texts often tell you to "get to know your character" by writing extensive biographies. This is only part of the battle. In script writing, we need to know not only who our characters are, but also how our characters relate to other people – how they interact. This is where status comes into play. When you combine a portrait of a character with an understanding of that character's preferred status role from community to community and her effectiveness in taking on each role, you can begin to predict how that character will act in almost any situation.

● **LESSON 8: SCRIPT ANALYSIS EXERCISE**

NOTE: Beginning and intermediate writers should do this exercise with an established play or screenplay. See the Appendix for a list of suggestions. Advanced writers have the option of bringing in their own scripts for review.

Have the group watch the same play or attend the same film. Get copies of the script to review.

For Discussion:

1. Identify each of the central characters. What was each character's overall status preference?
2. How flexible was each character with his status role?
3. Under what circumstances, in what situations, or with what people did each character try to play high status? How effective was he in taking on that high status role?
4. Under what circumstances, in what situations, or with what people did each character play low status? How effective was he in taking on that low status role?
5. Did any character start the story with one status and end it with a different one? If so, where exactly was the change? What caused the change?

LESSON 8: BEGINNER EXERCISE ▲

In this drill, you will generate two different original characters. You may use any of the following exercises as a starting point:

1. Write a three- to five-page biography of your character. Include an overview of family history; relationship history; significant life experiences; political leanings; religious beliefs; work experience; and financial standing.

2. Imagine that you are able to sneak into your character's home. Explore the home. Write a three- to five-page description of the home and what you find inside it.

3. Use the Solo Exercise at the end of Lesson Three to create a monologue for an original character.

4. Imagine that you are a private investigator. You must follow your character for a week and record his activity. Write a three- to five-page report of what you observe during that week. Where does the character go? Who does she talk to? Is any of her activity surprising or suspicious?

5. Make a collage of images that capture your character's personality.

After you have generated two new characters, write the answers to the following questions:

- Under what circumstances, in what environments, and with what people does each character try to play high status?
- Under what circumstances, in what environments, and with what people does each character try to play low status?
- In each of these situations, how effective is each character at taking on his preferred status position?

For Discussion:

Share your characters with the group.

1. What new insights or revelations did you get about each character as a result of this exercise? What was surprising or interesting?

2. In terms of the two characters' status preferences: In what places or under what circumstances would the two characters complement each other? In what places or under what circumstances would the two characters have a tacit agreement about their status roles?

3. In terms of the two characters' status preferences: In what places or under what circumstances would the two characters have friction with each other? In what places or under what circumstances would the two characters have tension about their status roles?

4. If you wanted to write an interesting scene between these two characters, where would you set the scene? What would be the circumstances of the scene? Why would you make those choices?

LESSON 8: INTERMEDIATE AND ADVANCED EXERCISE

Do the Beginner Exercise above. After you have completed it, write a three- to five-page dialogue between the two characters that you have created.

For Discussion:

Read the scenes out loud to the group.

1. Under what circumstances did each character try to play high status? How effective was he in taking on that high status role? How flexible was he?

2. Under what circumstances did each character play low status? How effective was he in taking on that low status role? How flexible was he?

3. What did the status interactions tell you about each character's personality?

4. What did the status interactions tell you about the characters' relationship to each other?

5. What were the most engaging or enjoyable aspects of the dialogue? What role did status play in those aspects?

✦ LESSON 8: SOLO EXERCISE

1. Take a dialogue scene from an existing play or screenplay. Do a status profile of each character in the scene.

2. Under what circumstances, in what situations, or with what people did each character try to play high status? How effective was he in taking on that high status role? How flexible was he?

3. Under what circumstances, in what situations, or with what people did each character play low status? How effective was he in taking on that low status role? How flexible was he?

4. Look over the status profiles of each character. Pick at least one aspect of each and change it to something completely different.

5. Now, rewrite the scene to match the new status profile. How did the change in the status profile affect the scene? As an ongoing workout, experiment with different changes and new rewrites.

LESSON NINE:
Friends and Foes

As Good As It Gets

In his book, *Impro*, Keith Johnstone makes the very important observation that status interactions are not always adversarial. Consider the two lines of dialogue mentioned in an earlier lesson:

> PERSON A: I baked some chocolate chip cookies.

> PERSON B: Finally, you baked something that you didn't burn!

Person A is playing high status to Person B. But is Person B being insulting and rude? Or is he engaging

79

in friendly banter? You could read the line with either interpretation.

As we discussed in the previous chapters, characters jockey for status position on a constantly shifting playing field. From community to community, from moment to moment, the world attempts to impose different status roles. From community to community, from moment to moment, we attempt to take on different status roles. In this environment, where everyone maneuvers for status all the time, what is the difference between friends and foes?

Johnstone argues that friends treat status interactions as a game to be enjoyed rather than a confrontation to be fought out. In friendly interactions, we have a tacit agreement about what status roles we will play and under what circumstances we will play them.

Consider your best friend. When does he support you and lift you up? When does he tease you and knock you down a peg? On what topics does he defer to your expertise? On what topics do you defer to his? When do you enjoy competing with him for high status? When do you enjoy competing with him for low status?

Friendship is not a relationship devoid of status interactions. You have as many status interactions with friends as you have with foes. The difference is that you enjoy the status interactions with your friends.

These interactions entertain you and fulfill your status needs from moment to moment.

In contrast, think about someone you dislike. What status roles does he attempt to take for himself? What status roles does he attempt to give you? To what things does he assign high status? To what things does he assign low status? Is there a difference between how he treats you and how you prefer to be treated? Is there a difference between the things he values and the things you value? I'm betting that there is.

When the status that someone else tries to impose doesn't match our own status needs, we get frustrated. Our conversation turns tense. The degree of tension depends on how entrenched we are in our preferred status positions and how tightly we hold on to them.

LESSON 9: SCRIPT ANALYSIS EXERCISE ●

Have each member of the group bring in a two- to three-page dialogue scene from an existing play or screenplay. (You can use the Appendix for suggestions or you can find material on your own.) Half of the group should bring in examples of friendly dialogue while the other half should bring in examples of tense or adversarial dialogue.

For Discussion

Review each scene with the group.

1. Overall, would you describe the characters in this scene as friendly toward each other? Or would you describe them as tense or adversarial toward each other?
2. To what things does each character assign high status? To what things does each character assign low status?
3. Are the characters in agreement on this?
4. Focus on one character in the scene. What status role does he try to take? What status role does the other character(s) appearing in the scene try to give him?
5. Are the characters in agreement on this?
6. Look at all the scenes from the group. Arrange them on a line from most friendly to most adversarial. Compare and contrast the friendly scenes to each other. What was the difference between a very friendly scene and a moderately friendly scene? Compare and contrast the adversarial scenes to each other. What was the difference between a very adversarial scene and a moderately adversarial scene?

▲ **LESSON 9: BEGINNER EXERCISE**

1. Go through the newspaper and pick out a story from any section. Create two characters who are interested in that story. Randomly assign each

character a status preference (very low status, low status, high status, or very high status).

2. Write a three- to five-page dialogue in which two characters discuss the subject of the news article. In the dialogue, keep the characters in their preferred status roles, but make the status interactions between the characters adversarial.

3. Rewrite the same dialogue making the status interactions between the characters friendly. (Make sure to keep the characters in their preferred status roles even as they are being friendly to each other.)

For Discussion:

Read both versions of each author's scene aloud to the group.

1. Which version is friendly? Which version is adversarial?

2. What in the dialogue made you understand that?

3. What specific changes did the author make in the rewrite to change the tone of the dialogue?

4. How did conflict or agreement about status roles contribute to the friendliness or tension of the dialogue?

■ LESSON 9: INTERMEDIATE AND ADVANCED EXERCISE

1. Go to any store. It might be a grocery store, a drugstore, a department store, or an online store. Pick out one item that is for sale.

2. You will write five different versions of a two-to four-page dialogue in which two or more characters discuss this item. Before you begin, randomly assign each character a status preference (very low status, low status, high status, or very high status).

3. In the first version of the dialogue, make the relationships between the characters as tension filled or as adversarial as possible. With each of the following five rewrites, make the relationships slightly friendlier. Even as the dialogue gets friendlier with each rewrite, each character must still maintain his preferred status role.

For Discussion:

Read all five versions of each author's scene aloud to the group.

1. Have the group rank the scenes from most adversarial/tension filled to friendliest.

2. What in the dialogue helped you make your ranking choices?

3. What specific changes did the author make in each rewrite to change the tone of the dialogue?

4. How did conflict or agreement about status roles contribute to the friendliness or tension of the dialogue?

LESSON 9: **SOLO EXERCISE**   ✚

1. Put the numbers one through ten on slips of paper and place them in a hat. In this exercise, the numbers will represent a spectrum of friendliness to antagonism. Ten is very, very, very, very friendly. One is very, very, very, very adversarial. Five is about halfway in between.

2. Draw three numbers out of the hat.

3. Go to a random web page. You can either find a random page yourself, or you can get directed to a random page through a site such as *www.randomwebsite.com.*

4. Inspired by the content of that random web page, write a three- to five-page scene between two characters. Write the scene so that the dialogue starts out at the friendliness level of the first number, moves to the level of the second number, and then finishes at the level of the third number. Make sure to use status conflicts and agreements to create the tension and friendliness in the dialogue.

5. Repeat this exercise regularly as an ongoing writer's workout.

LESSON TEN:
Tools

Fight Club

L ike other mammals, humans use a variety of physical cues to communicate what status they are playing. A straight spine, squared shoulders, and a straight-forward gaze are signs of someone playing high status. A slouched spine, hunched shoulders, and a downward gaze are signs of someone playing low status. These mimic actions seen all over the animal kingdom. High status orangutans stand and beat their chests to assert dominance. When my late beagle got caught eating from the table, she would hang her head and crouch low to the ground — a sign of submission.

In the animal kingdom, the strongest and healthiest animals take on high status roles. The remainder of the pack falls into lower status positions. This social arrangement works for animals. Animals have very basic needs: food, good mates, and defense from predators. For animals, health and fitness are the primary requirements for survival. But what about human communities? We don't only need food, good mates, and defense from predators. We also need to build bridges, enjoy music, share knowledge, and accomplish an infinite number of other tasks to maintain our society. For us, we don't always need the strongest or the fittest to be in charge. Sometimes we need to put the smartest in charge, or the most diplomatic, or the most musically talented, or the best teachers, or the most patient listeners, or the most spiritually enlightened, or... the list goes on and on.

Because our large, complicated brains evolved sophisticated language skills, created an infinite number of different communities, and invented everything from sports cars to boxer shorts to nuclear weapons, our ways of showing status are far more diverse than any other creature on the planet. We aren't limited to roaring and beating our chests to show high status. We buy huge expensive cars, show off our understanding of current events, or play loud banging drum solos in a rock'n'roll band. We aren't limited to cringing and slouching to show low status. We send fawning greeting cards, listen attentively as someone else explains current events, or scream adulation at our favorite movie star as he walks down the red carpet.

In fact, there are as many different ways of displaying high status or low status as there are different human communities on the face of the planet. As part of its attempt to define status to its members, a community will create status tools: special environments, objects, powers, rituals, or responsibilities that broadcast and maintain the status roles of its members.

When I taught in my former classroom, the community of the Northwestern University Theater Department put me in a high status role. I was the person with authority; I was the person who could demand things from everyone else in the room. I had the power to assert my will in the classroom. The university community helped me accomplish this by giving me some high status tools, most notably the power to control my students' grades. If I needed to push a student in line, I didn't have to beat my chest like an orangutan (although, sometimes, I wanted to); I simply needed to threaten the student with a failing grade. It was the university equivalent of beating my chest. It was how I displayed high status within this small human community. And it only worked in this particular community. Threatening a judge with a failing grade has never gotten me anywhere in traffic court, for example.

On the other hand, if I get pulled over for speeding, I am in an innately low status position. The community has given the police officer some high status tools (the ability to write me a ticket, the ability to arrest me, the gun) to keep me in line.

As a writer, you should start paying attention to how status manifests itself in different communities. Look for the status tools: the special environments, objects, powers, rituals, or responsibilities that each community creates. What do these things say about a community's values? How might characters use these tools to try to control status?

● LESSON 10: SCRIPT ANALYSIS EXERCISE

Have the group watch the same film or see the same play. (See the Appendix for a list of suggestions.) Try to pick a film or play that is set in a world very different than your own. It might feature a different culture, age group, race, socioeconomic background, workplace, or time period. Whatever it is, the environment should be dramatically different than the one you experience day to day.

For Discussion:

1. To what values and ideas does this community

assign high status? What in the production made you think this?

2. To what values and ideas does this community assign low status? What in the production made you think this?

3. To whom does this community assign high status? What in the production made you think this?

4. To whom does the community assign low status? What in the production made you think this?

5. What special environments, objects, rituals, powers, and responsibilities does the community use to impose and maintain status roles?

6. Does any character in the script have a different understanding of status or a different vision for what values should be given high status or low status? If so, who is it? How does that difference manifest itself in the character's actions? How does that difference manifest itself in the character's dialogue?

7. How does all of this compare and contrast to your own world? Where are the similarities? Where are the differences?

LESSON 10: BEGINNER EXERCISE ▲

1. Research or visit a community that is very different from your own. It could be a community

from another culture or time, or a community characterized by an age group, profession, or gender that differs from your own. In this exercise, it will help you to be as specific and narrow as possible in defining the community. (For example, the community of women at the ritzy hair salon will give you more specific results than the community of all the women who live in New Hampshire.) Analyze the status tools and rituals of the community.

2. Write a three- to five-page dialogue between three people in this community.

For Discussion:

Review the scenes with the group. For each scene, discuss the following questions:

1. To whom does this community assign high status? What in the dialogue made you think this?

2. To whom does this community assign low status? What in the dialogue made you think this?

3. To what values and ideas does this community assign high status? What in the dialogue made you think this?

4. To what values and ideas does this community assign low status? What in the dialogue made you think this?

5. What special environments, objects, rituals, powers, and responsibilities does the community use to impose and maintain status roles?

LESSON 10: INTERMEDIATE AND ADVANCED EXERCISE

We've been talking a lot about dialogue, but it's important to remember that status interactions don't just take place with words. In many cases, status interactions are physical. Even without dialogue, characters are able to utilize the status tools of a community. The CEO gets the biggest office. A celebrity is trailed by his entourage. The president of the United States enters a room and citizens stand. All of these things wordlessly communicate high status. A sports fan waits in line for her hero's autograph. A defendant sits on a chair lower than the judge's dais. The devout bow or kneel in prayer. All of these things wordlessly communicate low status. In this exercise, you will practice writing status interactions without dialogue.

1. Do step 1 of the Beginner Exercise in this lesson.
2. Write a two- to three-page script that takes place in the community you've selected. The script must be completely *without* dialogue. Use only stage directions and actions to communicate status interactions.

For Discussion:

Review the scenes with the group. For each scene, discuss the following questions:

1. To whom does this community assign high status? What in the script made you think this?

2. To whom does this community assign low status? What in the script made you think this?

3. To what values and ideas does this community assign high status? What in the script made you think this?

4. To what values and ideas does this community assign low status? What in the script made you think this?

5. What objects, rituals, powers, and responsibilities does the community use to impose and maintain status roles?

✛ LESSON 10: SOLO EXERCISE

1. Select an existing dialogue scene from a play or screenplay. Adapt and rewrite the scene to take place in a completely different setting. For example, you might change the location, culture, or time period. As you write, you should try to keep the characters as faithful as possible to their original status roles, while updating dialogue, the environment, and the status rituals to

the new setting. (If you're confused about how this works, compare the film *Emma* (1996) to the film *Clueless* (1995). *Clueless* is an adaptation of *Emma*. *Clueless* takes the original characters from *Emma*, and maintains their plot and status roles, but places the whole story in a completely different world).

2. Repeat this exercise regularly as an ongoing writer's workout.

THE SCENE: DIALOGUE WITH DIRECTION

LESSON ELEVEN:
Setting the Scene

The Wizard of Oz

haracters don't exist in a vacuum. They exist in an environment. Some kind of world exists outside of your character's self. As part of your writing process, you need to determine what that world is. You need to understand it in detail.

When people talk about writing, they frequently zero in on the importance of character. Every writing

99

TALK THE TALK ■ PENNISTON

book I've ever read discusses how important it is to understand every facet of a character's personality and every nuance of his life. It's true. Character is important. However, a character's environment brings as much life and meaning to your script as a character's self. This is a strangely neglected fact in the discussion of scriptwriting. I read many scripts in which interesting characters inhabit dull, stereotypical, or poorly defined worlds. This is particularly true when I teach actors how to write. With their training, actors are good at understanding the depth and complexity of people. They have had less practice in thinking about the depth and complexity of a character's environment. As a writer, you need to approach your character's world with the same curiosity, open-mindedness, and commitment to discovering detail and nuance as you use when exploring your character's psychology.

To make this issue more complicated, you need to understand that characters don't just inhabit worlds. They inhabit worlds within worlds. If I were to ask you to describe the world that I live in, where would you start? By describing planet Earth? Or the United States of America? Would you focus in more closely and describe the Midwest, or the city of Chicago? Even within Chicago, I inhabit many worlds. There is the world of the office in which I work. There is the world of the church that I attend. There is the world of my marriage to my husband. There is the world of my home, which in turn holds the worlds of my dining room, my living room, my bedroom, and my kitchen. There are worlds that I visit, such as the world of a Caribbean resort, or that of the Nepalese family I lived with when I traveled after college. Then, there are also worlds that are part of my universe, but that I've never been inside, such as that of Pennsylvania coal miners, for example. I've also never been inside the world of British Parliament, French fashion, or that of the stranger sitting next to me on the train last week.

I have a fundamentally different relationship to each of these worlds. Each has its own personality, set of rules, vocabulary, and culture. It is a common mistake among new scriptwriters to ignore these differences.

LESSON 11: SCRIPT ANALYSIS EXERCISE   ●

NOTE: Beginning and intermediate writers should do this exercise with an established play or screenplay. See the Appendix for a list of suggestions. Advanced writers have the option of bringing in their own material for analysis.

Have the group watch the same film, attend the same play, or read the same script.

For Discussion:

1. What world is the story set in? Give it a name. Be as specific as possible.

2. What are the larger worlds that this world is a part of? What are the smaller worlds contained within this world? Identify what it was within the script that led you to these conclusions.

3. Describe the setting and situation of this world. What is its time and place? Give a detailed description of what this world looks like. What do you see when you walk around this world? What do you hear? What do you smell? What do you feel? What kinds of clothes are people wearing? How do people talk? What is the day-to-day activity of this world?

4. Who are the inhabitants of this world? Who do you see when you walk around this world? What are they doing?

5. What defines status in this world? Who or what has the highest status? Who or what has the lowest? Identify moments within the script that led you to these conclusions.

6. What is the tone of this world? What emotions does it evoke? Identify elements of the script that evoke those tones and emotions.

7. Are there any special or unique rules that govern the way this world works? Identify what it was within the script that led you to these conclusions.

8. How is this world different than your own? How is it similar?

LESSON 11: **BEGINNER EXERCISE** ▲

You are an explorer. Your job is to identify a world and to map it out.

1. Give a name to this world. Does it exist in a real or imaginary location, such as the "World of Buckingham Palace," the "World of My Mother's Beauty Salon," or the "World of Planet Krypton"? Does it exist among a particular set of people (real or imaginary), such as the "World of Secret Agents" or the "World of Talking Mice"? Is it the world of a particular person, such as the "World of Martin Luther King, Jr.," or the "World of Luke Skywalker"? Is it an abstract concept or organizing principle, such as the "World of Computer Technology," or the "World of Republican Foreign Policy"? Does the world exist at a particular time, such as the "World of September 11, 2001" or the "World of the Fifth-Century A.D." or the "World of Star Date 3456.23"? Perhaps the world can be described by a combination of these factors: the "World of Computer Technology at the Pentagon on September 11, 2001," for example.

2. Identify the larger worlds that this world is a part of. Identify the smaller worlds contained within this world.

3. Describe the setting and situation of this world. What is its time and place? Write a detailed description of what this world looks like. What do you see when you walk around this world? What do you hear? What do you smell? What do you feel? What kinds of clothes are people wearing? How do people talk? What is the day-to-day activity of this world?
4. Who are the inhabitants of this world? Whom do you see when you walk around this world? What are they doing?
5. What defines status in this world? Who or what has the highest status? Who or what has the lowest?
6. What is the tone of this world? What emotions does it evoke?
7. Are there any special or unique rules that govern the way this world works?
8. Repeat steps 2 through 7. Add more detail.
9. Create a collage of words and images that you might associate with this world.

For Discussion:

Have each author share her collage and do a ten-minute presentation on her world to the group.

1. Have members of the group question the author on the details of the world. Try to fill in any blanks.

2. What is familiar about this world? What aspects of it do you relate to?

3. What is unfamiliar or foreign about this world? What aspects of it are outside the realm of your own experience?

4. What is most interesting or intriguing to you about this world?

5. How do you feel about this world? What would it be like for you to enter it?

6. If you were writing a scene set within this world, where would you begin?

LESSON 11: INTERMEDIATE AND ADVANCED EXERCISE

Do the Beginner Exercise (without the discussion). Write a three- to five-page dialogue that is set within this world.

For Discussion:

Read the dialogues out loud to the group. *Do not* share the world notes or the collage with the group. Based on each dialogue, have members of the group try to answer the following questions:

1. What are the larger worlds that this world is a part of? What are the smaller worlds contained within this world? If these details weren't explicit, what in the script caused you to draw these conclusions?

2. Describe the setting and situation of this world. What is its time and place? Give a detailed description of what this world looks like. What do you see when you walk around this world? What do you hear? What do you smell? What do you feel? What kinds of clothes are people wearing? How do people talk? What is the day-to-day activity of this world? If these details weren't explicit, what in the script caused you to draw these conclusions?

3. Who are the inhabitants of this world? Whom do you see when you walk around this world? What are they doing? If these details weren't explicit, what in the script caused you to draw these conclusions?

4. What defines status in this world? Who or what has the highest status? Who or what has the lowest? If these details weren't explicit, what in the script caused you to draw these conclusions?

5. What is the tone of this world? What emotions does it evoke? If these details weren't explicit, what in the script caused you to draw these conclusions?

6. Are there any special or unique rules that govern the way this world works? If these details weren't explicit, what in the script caused you to draw these conclusions?

7. Have each writer describe how the group's impressions matched his own intentions.

8. Were there any differences between what the writer intended and what the group inferred? If so, why?

9. Have each writer discuss how the exercise in creating the world inspired or influenced the dialogue.

LESSON 11: SOLO EXERCISE   ✚

As a regular writer's workout, do the Beginner Exercise in this chapter. Create a permanent file for each world that you develop with this exercise. In the future, when you are working on scenes or full-length scripts, you can refer back to these files for setting ideas and inspiration.

LESSON TWELVE:
Populating the Scene

It's time to meet the characters in your scene. Who are they?

A character is a person, and — just as there is for a real person — there is a process for getting to know him. You meet him for the first time; you get a first impression. Then, as you spend more time with him, you become more intimate. You go to his house; you meet his family; you see what he likes to do for fun. You hang out with him in different situations and you learn things: whether he has a short temper, how much he drinks, what he likes to eat for breakfast. If you spend enough time with a character, you will be able to give as much detail about his life and personality as you could if you were talking about your best friend.

Just like real people, some characters will interest you more than others. These are the ones you should pursue and find out more about; these are the ones who will eventually end up in your scripts.

You should make notes on all the characters you start to develop. You never know where the characters will end up. You might create a minor character for an assignment and then find he takes on a life of his own to become the center of an entire script. A character who starts out as a sketchy and unusable idea for one project might find a full life in a different project.

As a writer, you must know as much as you possibly can about your characters. This process starts from the moment a character enters your consciousness. It intensifies as you start writing about him. It becomes a team effort when your script goes into production; even after that, it dwindles, but it doesn't stop. I'm still learning things about characters I wrote years ago.

LESSON 12: EXERCISE INTRODUCTION

For the exercises in this chapter, you are a spy. You are a top-level secret agent. Your assignment is to gather all the knowledge you can about your character. You will be sent on several missions. Through these missions, you will develop a character file for a particular character. This character file will contain two sections:

1. **Field notes:** Your field notes should include only behavior and facts that you have witnessed on your missions. Do not draw any conclusions. Do not say that "Bob loves his mother." Instead, report on Bob's behavior toward his mother: He brings her flowers on her birthday, he calls her every night, he takes her out to the theater, etc.

Do not say that "Elaine is secretly the parent of an illegitimate child." Instead, report exactly what you observed or what document you uncovered that reveals that Elaine is the parent of an illegitimate child.

2. **Profile reports:** In this section, you should write up the conclusions that you have drawn about your character based on your observations. In particular, look for patterns of behavior that indicate an attitude about or relationship with a particular topic. Every conclusion must be linked to facts or observations that you have detailed somewhere in your field notes.

There are three secrets to being a successful secret agent:

1. *Use detail.* Take thorough notes on each mission; include as much detail as possible. Explain exactly what you saw and where you saw it. When you have completed your notes, go back and add more detail.

2. *Be proactive.* Your boss has sent you on a mission, but you're not limited to answering only the questions that the boss asks. Be proactive in digging for information. When you discover something interesting, unusual, or unexplained about the character, zero in on that fact and

do further research. If necessary, create another mission for yourself that has the sole purpose of researching that fact.

3. *Be creative.* You are the world's best secret agent. You can gather information by any means necessary. You are not only an expert locksmith and a master of disguise, but you also have the ability to become invisible and to travel through time. You can break into buildings and dig through files. You can follow the character without being seen. You can observe any moment in the character's life. You can don a disguise and interview a character or his friends. (If you do an imaginary interview with a character or his friends, write it up word for word and put it in your field notes.)

▲ LESSON 12: BEGINNER EXERCISE

Go on Missions 1 through 4 below. As discussed in the exercise introduction, take field notes and prepare a profile report.

• **Mission 1**: Research basic information about this character. Give his full name and nickname (if he has one). How old is this person? When and where was he born? Where does he live now? Does he live with other people, like friends or family? Who are the five most significant people in his life? What's his current job? What's his financial situation? What does he look like? Give a detailed physical description. Include any other facts that you think are relevant.

- **Mission 2:** Go to the character's house. Give a detailed description of the outside of the house. Break into the house. Give a detailed description of each room. Your boss wants to know everything about the house. How are the rooms decorated? What's on the shelves? What's in the drawers? What food is in the pantry? What clothes are in the closet?

- **Mission 3**: Follow the character around for one week. List and describe in detail everywhere that the character goes. Identify everyone whom the character talks to.

- **Mission 4**: Find out about the character's history. Where is he from? What was his childhood like? What kind of education did he receive? Has he ever moved? If so, where and why? What have been the major turning points in the character's life?

For Discussion:

Based on your field notes and profile report, prepare a ten-minute presentation on your character for the group. What are the major conclusions that you have drawn about your character? What did you witness that led you to these conclusions? After the group has heard the report, discuss it.

1. What facts or aspects of the character does the group find the most interesting?
2. What facts or aspects of the character does the group find surprising?
3. Based on the facts presented, what additional assumptions might be drawn about the character?
4. Based on the facts presented, does anyone in the group have a differing opinion on the character?
5. What questions about the character arise as a result of the presentation? If you were spying on this character, what information would you gather next?

■ **LESSON 12: INTERMEDIATE AND ADVANCED EXERCISE**

Go on Missions 1 through 4 in the Beginner Exercise. In addition, pick four more missions from the list below:

• **Mission 5:** Go undercover and interview one or more of the people whom the character has talked to in the last week. Get each person talking about the character. Have each person tell you about his relationship with the character. How did they first meet? How long have they known each other?

Do they have any interesting memories about the character? Any good stories? Transcribe this imaginary interview word for word.

- **Mission 6:** Go back to the character's hometown. Interview people from the character's childhood. (Some suggestions include the character's parents, the character's siblings, the character's grade school teacher, the character's high school sweetheart, and the character's best friend while he was growing up.) Get each of those people to tell you about their relationship with the character. How did they first meet? How long have they known each other? Do they have any interesting memories about the character? Any good stories? Are they still in touch with the character? If not, why?

- **Mission 7:** Go to each of the places that the character has lived. Interview people who knew him from those places. For example, if the character was in the Army, interview his best Army buddy and his commanding officer.

- **Mission 8:** Research and report on the character's religious education, beliefs, and practices. What was the character taught about God? What does the character think about God now? Conduct interviews if necessary.

- **Mission 9:** Research and report on the character's sense of ethics. It might be helpful to go to times and places where the character has faced an ethical dilemma and report on how he handled it. Has the character's sense of ethics undergone any significant changes over the course of his life? If so, when and why? Conduct interviews if necessary.

- **Mission 10:** Research and report on the character's financial situation, attitude about money, and spending habits. Has the character's financial situation, attitude about money, or spending habits undergone any significant changes over the course of his life? If so, when and why? Conduct interviews if necessary.

- **Mission 11:** Research and report on the character's social and political beliefs. Are there any social causes that the character fights for or believes in? Have the character's social and political beliefs undergone any significant changes over the course of his life so far? If so, when and why? Conduct interviews if necessary.

- **Mission 12:** Research and report on the relationship that the character has with each of the five most significant people in his life. Have those relationships undergone any significant changes over the course of his life so far? If so, when and why? Conduct interviews if necessary.

- **Mission 13:** Research and report on the character's hobbies and interests. What does he like to do in his free time? How and when did he first become interested in his hobby? How obsessive is he about it? How does it fit into the rest of his life? Conduct interviews if necessary.

- **Mission 14:** Research and report on the character's professional life. What is his job? How does he feel about his job? What do others think of him at work? How good is he at his job? What particular skills does the character bring to the job? Has the character's professional life undergone any significant changes since he started working? If so, when and why? Conduct interviews if necessary.

- **Mission 15:** Research and report on the character's relationship with his body. Does the character have any health problems or physical disabilities? Report on any particular physical indulgences, passions, or addictions (food, sex, drugs, alcohol, etc.). Has the character's relationship with his body changed over the course of his life so far? If so, when and why? Conduct interviews if necessary.

- **Mission 16:** Research and report on the character's status profile. In what situations does the character play high status? In what situations does the character play low status? How comfortable is the character in each status role? How effective is the character at taking on each status role? Has the character's status profile changed over the course of his life so far? If so, when and why?

- **Mission 17**: Interview your character. Here are some suggested interview questions, but you should feel free to add your own: Describe your five most vivid memories. Describe the five most significant things that have happened to you in your life so far. What do you hope to accomplish within the next year? Type up the interview word for word and report on any conclusions that you draw.

For Discussion:

Based on your field notes and profile report, prepare a fifteen- to twenty-minute presentation on your character to the group. What are the major conclusions that you have drawn about your character? What did you witness that led you to these conclusions? After the group has heard the report, discuss it.

1. What facts or aspects of the character does the group find the most interesting?
2. What facts or aspects of the character does the group find surprising?
3. Based on the facts presented, what additional assumptions might be drawn about the character?
4. Based on the facts presented, does anyone in the group have a differing opinion on the character?

5. What questions about the character arise as a result of the presentation? If you were spying on this character, what information would you gather next?

LESSON 12: SOLO EXERCISE   ✚

1. Conduct more research into your character. If you have discovered any fact that seems significant, unusual, or unexplained, create a new mission to research it. You can research any facet of your character that interests you. You might research your character's obsession with baseball, his fetish for women's feet, his television watching habits, or his secret stash of romance novels. To make your missions effective, try to stay focused on one topic at a time. In doing your research, examine not only the topic at this moment in the character's life, but also the character's history with the topic. Has his relationship with the topic ever changed? If so, when and why?

2. As a regular writer's workout, repeat the Beginner, Intermediate, and Solo Exercises for new characters that you develop. Create a permanent file for each character. In the future, when you are working on scenes or full-length scripts, you can refer back to these files for ideas and inspiration.

● LESSON 12: SCRIPT ANALYSIS EXERCISE

NOTE: Beginning and intermediate writers should do this exercise with an established play or screenplay. See the Appendix for a list of suggestions. Advanced writers have the option of bringing in their own material for analysis.

1. Have the group watch the same film, attend the same play, or read the same script. Within that script, the group should agree on one central character to analyze.

2. After selecting the character, have each member of the group choose a different mission from the Beginner and Intermediate/Advanced Exercises presented in this lesson.

3. Have each member of the group prepare field notes and a profile report for his mission. One rule: While on your mission, you must limit yourself *only* to information contained within the script. Unlike the previous exercises, you cannot do interviews or jump into times, places, or scenes outside of the world of the script. You must limit yourself to observing only what the play or film presents.

4. Have each member of the group share his profile report in a five-minute presentation.

For Discussion:

For each presentation, discuss:

1. For your mission, how difficult was it to find information in the script?
2. Was everything in the profile report substantiated by something contained within the existing script? Make sure that the person presenting the report identifies something specific within the script to back up each assumption and conclusion.

After everyone has presented, discuss:

1. What facts or aspects of the character does the group find the most interesting?
2. What facts or aspects of the character does the group find surprising?
3. Based on the facts presented, what additional assumptions might be drawn about the character?
4. Based on the facts presented, does anyone in the group have a differing opinion on the character?

ROSENCRANTZ: Now why exactly are you behaving in this extraordinary manner?
–Tom Stoppard (*Rosencrantz & Guildenstern Are Dead*)

LESSON THIRTEEN:
Crafting the Line

I am going to begin this chapter with a physics metaphor. Please, *do not panic*. Even if you're like me and you became a writer precisely because you couldn't cut it in math or science, hang in there. I promise to keep it simple.

Imagine a duck swimming in the river. The duck swims straight toward shore.

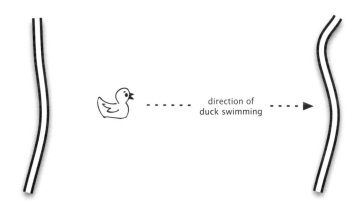

direction of duck swimming

The duck paddles in one direction. However, the river also has a strong current downstream.

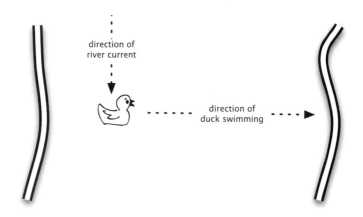

Now, what happens to the path of the duck?

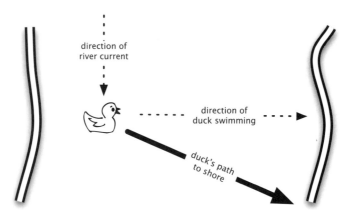

The duck swims perpendicular to shore, but the current pushes the duck downstream at the same time. As a result, the duck travels to the shoreline in a diagonal path. This is a living example of Newton's second law of motion. That law states what many of us know to be true intuitively: An object's movement can be determined by the sum of all forces acting upon it.

The duck pushes itself in one direction; the current pushes it in a different direction; the result is a path that reflects the combination of both forces.

What does this have to do with dialogue? Dialogue isn't just conversation; it's conversation in motion. Dialogue moves from one place to another. And, because it moves, we can find a very useful metaphor in Newton's laws of motion. Using Newton, here's a working definition of what makes a good line of dialogue:

> A good line of dialogue manifests the sum of all forces (both internal and external) acting on a character at a particular moment.

To understand how this law plays out in your writing, imagine the following two scenes:

> Scene 1: Your character is a lifelong Democrat. He hates the Republican party and everything it stands for. There is a knock on the door. A woman has come to solicit contributions for the Republican party. The woman is a complete stranger. What does your character say to her?

> Scene 2: Your character is a lifelong Democrat. He hates the Republican party and everything it stands for. There is a knock on the door. A woman has come to solicit contributions for the Republican party. The

woman is your character's childhood sweetheart — a love that he has dreamed about
rekindling for the last two decades. What
does your character say to her?

In Scene 1, the Republican is a complete stranger.
Your character can say or do whatever he wants without fear of retribution. He might say, "Go to hell," or
he might just give a curt, "I'm not interested." Whatever he says, the only force acting on him is the desire
to tell the solicitor no and to make her go away.

In Scene 2, the Republican is your character's childhood sweetheart. A competing force is now in the mix.
On the one hand, your character wants to communicate that he's not interested in making a donation.
On the other hand, he wants to rekindle a romance.
The character will adjust his response to reflect those
competing forces. He probably won't say, "Go to hell,"
or give a curt, "I'm not interested." He will temper
his response to be warmer and more respectful. If he
values the woman more than he values his politics, he
might even cave in and make the donation.

● **LESSON 13: SCRIPT ANALYSIS EXERCISE**

Have the group attend the same play or watch the same
movie. (See the Appendix for a list of suggestions.) Get
copies of the script for the group to review.

Select one of the central characters. Have each

member of the group select a different line of dialogue from that character. After each group member selects the line, she will present an analysis of that line. In the analysis, she should answer the following questions:

1. What is the context for this line? What is happening in the script at this moment?
2. What are the specific forces (both external and internal) acting on the character in this moment?
3. Which of those forces are strongest? Which are weakest?
4. How did the line of dialogue reflect the balance of those forces?

For Discussion:

1. After each presentation, have the group weigh in with its perspective. Does the group agree with the analysis? Is there any disagreement? Was anything left out?
2. After everyone has presented, compare and contrast the forces acting on the character at different moments of the script. How are they similar? How are they different? What does that tell you about the character?

LESSON 13: BEGINNER EXERCISE ▲

In this drill, you will practice bending lines of dialogue to reflect multiple forces acting upon a character.

1. We will start with one neutral line of dialogue:

   MAN (to a woman): I'll see you at the conference this weekend.

   Now, rewrite the above line four different ways:
   - Man wants to start a long-term relationship with the woman.
   - Man wants to have a one-night stand with the woman.
   - Man wants the woman as a professional mentor.
   - Man wants the woman to come work for his company.

2. You now have four lines of dialogue. Rewrite each of them three different ways:
   - Man wants to seem smart.
   - Man wants to seem charming or funny.
   - Man wants to seem serious.

3. Take the resulting twelve lines of dialogue. Rewrite each of them two different ways:
   - Man wants to play high status.
   - Man wants to play low status

4. You now have twenty-four lines of dialogue. Rewrite each line to add a new force into the mix (create a different force for each line).

For Discussion:

After completing the exercise, you should have twenty-four lines of dialogue, each one reflecting a completely different mix of forces.

1. Have a writer read one of his lines. Have the group try to identify all the forces acting on the character in the line.
2. Have the writer read a different one of his lines. Have the group try to identify how the forces are different.
3. Repeat steps 1 and 2 so that each writer has a chance to share his work.
4. Have the group discuss the process for crafting the lines. What made the assignment easy? What made it difficult?
5. Did the addition of different forces change your perception of the character you were writing? Did it open up possibilities that you hadn't considered? Did it ever limit you in ways you found frustrating?
6. If you were to use one of your lines as the jumping-off point for a scene, which one would it be? Why?

■ LESSON 13: INTERMEDIATE AND ADVANCED EXERCISE

1. Start with the following two lines of dialogue:

   CHARACTER A: I'm going to the store.

   CHARACTER B: Get some milk while you're there.

2. Rewrite Character A's line three times. Each time, add an additional force acting on Character A. You may choose whatever forces you'd like.

3. Rewrite Character B's line three times. Each time, add an additional force acting on Character B. You may choose whatever forces you'd like.

4. Take the last line of the Character A and B rewrites. Use those lines as the first two lines of a one- to two-page dialogue between the two characters. Try to keep the initial forces consistent through the entire dialogue.

For Discussion:

Read each dialogue out loud.

1. Have the group try to identify the forces acting upon each character.

2. How did different combinations of starting forces lead to creating different character personalities, different relationships, and different scenes?

3. For each dialogue, discuss whether the forces stayed consistent over the course of the whole scene. If not, when did they change?

4. If the author changed the combination of forces over the course of the dialogue, have the author discuss why that happened. Why wasn't he able to maintain the consistency of the forces?

LESSON 13: SOLO EXERCISE ✚

Watch a play or a film. Pick out a line of dialogue from that script.

1. Identify all of the forces acting on the character in that moment of dialogue.

2. Rewrite the line of dialogue at least five different times. Each time, completely change the forces acting on the character in that moment.

3. Write down a list of effects that this new line of dialogue might have on the scene or the story. How might this revision lead to changes in the script? Would it alter the plot? Would it alter a character relationship? Would it change your perception of a character's personality?

4. Repeat this exercise as an ongoing writer's workout.

MARGO: Fasten your seatbelts. It's going to be a bumpy night.
—*All About Eve* (1950)

LESSON FOURTEEN:
From Line to Line

All About Eve

et's start with a simple observation: Plays and films are experienced over a period of time. They are not instantaneous events. They last. Sometimes they last for five minutes, sometimes for eight hours, but they always last for some unit of time.

So you go into a theater, you sit in the dark, the

curtain rises (or the film starts) and... What happens? What exactly happens?

Things change. On a fundamental level, when you are watching a play or a film, you are watching a series of changes. If things didn't change, the curtain would go up, you'd see the actors and... they'd stand there, frozen, perfectly still, forever.

Not so interesting, eh?

As a scriptwriter, your first job is to make things change. All of the performing arts have addressed this problem in some way. Musicians change sounds from moment to moment. Dancers change their bodies from moment to moment. Because scriptwriters create a whole universe, our palette is bigger. Unlike musicians and dancers, we aren't limited to simply changing sounds or movement; we can also change dialogue, costumes, lighting, sets, and props. We can change character actions, character relationships, and character situations. We can change the perception of ideas, themes, and images. We can change the laws of physics, the nature of good and evil, or the use of the word "sprinkle."

The discussion of when and why to change things is something we will take up in later chapters. For now, let's consider *how* to change things. For this, we will return to our physics metaphor (again, *stay calm*, I promise to keep it simple).

In physics, to change the motion of an object, you change the balance of forces acting upon that object. If our duck is swimming toward shore and, suddenly, a gale force wind comes along, the duck will be blown off course. The shift in the balance of forces creates a shift in motion. Similarly, a shift in the balance of forces acting on a character will cause a character to change direction.

Writers have lots of different names for these moments of shifting forces: turning points, plot points, events, decisions, key moments, etc. Whatever term one uses, the important thing to remember is that these moments don't arise out of nowhere. They always mark a shift in the balance of forces underlying the action of the script. Each shift creates a clear dividing line between "before" and "after."

Let's move our imaginary classroom to game six of the 1998 NBA finals: the Chicago Bulls vs. the Utah Jazz.

> With nineteen seconds left in the game, the Utah Jazz are up by one point. Anticipating victory, the crowd in Utah is going wild. Their star player, Karl Malone, has the ball and is charging down the court to widen the lead. Then, like a stealth bomber, legendary Bulls player Michael Jordan jets in from behind and strips the ball from Malone.

Jordan drives down the court and nails an eighteen-foot jump shot from the top of the key with five seconds left on the clock. The Jazz fans moan with one astonished gasp and fall silent. Here in Chicago, the city goes wild. Bulls win 87-86.

Compare that description of the game to this one:

With some time left to go in the game (no one knows how much), one team or the other is ahead (no one knows which one; we lost track). The crowd in Utah is scratching their heads, asking each other what is going on. Some guy on the floor takes the ball from another guy. However, no one is wearing uniforms, so we're not sure which teams the guys are on. The guy who took the ball charges down the court and shoots the ball, but we can't quite see if it goes through the net. A few people cheer. A few people boo. The rest of us wonder what's going on. We see the players leave the court and we belatedly realize that the game is over. We ask the other people at the stadium which team won. No one is sure.

So... which experience is more satisfying as a spectator? In which experience do we get to ride the twists and turns and experience the emotional highs and lows of the game?

Sporting events are dramas. They are very simple dramas, but we can still learn something fundamental about storytelling from them: To make the experience of a story satisfying, you must make the shifts in forces crystal clear to an audience. As a group, the audience needs to understand:

- **The Situation:** "With nineteen seconds left in the game, the Utah Jazz are up by one point." In sports, we always know the lay of the land. At every moment, we understand the balance of forces with pinpoint precision. We know who's ahead. We know who's behind. We know how much time is on the clock. We know which team everyone is on. We understand the rules of the game.

- **The Moment of Change:** "Then, like a stealth bomber, legendary Bulls player Michael Jordan jets in from behind and strips the ball from Malone." There it is: the exact moment when the tide turns. Everyone recognizes it. Jazz fans scream together in dismay. Bulls fans leap to their feet in hope.

- **The New Situation Resulting from the Change:** "Jordan drives down the court and nails an eighteen-foot jump shot from the top of the key with five seconds left on the clock." As sports fans, we know, things are different than they were a few seconds ago. The Bulls have gone from one point down to one point up. With seconds to go, there is now almost no chance for the Jazz to recover. A few seconds ago, we anticipated a Jazz victory. Now we anticipate a Bulls victory. The balance of forces has shifted.

While plays, films, and sporting events are experienced over a period of time, change is experienced in an instant. When done well, it is a moment shared by the entire audience. In the most effective scripts, an audience laughs together, cries together, is surprised together, gasps together, realizes things together, and is horrified together. In the least effective scripts, a few people laugh while others wonder why they are laughing. Audience members scratch their heads and whisper questions to each other like, "Wait, did that guy just confess to the murder? Or was he talking about something else?" The difference between effective and ineffective writing is the clear communication of change. An audience, at all times, needs to understand a) what's going on; b) when what's going on changes; and c) how the new thing that's going on is fundamentally different than before.

Line by line, dialogue rides on a current of shifting forces. If the script is written well, each line of dialogue will reflect those shifts. In the dialogue, the audience will feel the undulating balance of forces in the script viscerally. When those forces shift, the audience will experience it together, in a single dramatic moment.

LESSON 14: SCRIPT ANALYSIS EXERCISE ●

Have the group attend the same play or watch the same movie. (See the Appendix for a list of suggestions.) Pick the most powerful or interesting dialogue scene. Review that scene with the group.

For Discussion:

1. Go through the scene character by character. Identify all the forces acting on each character.

2. In what ways do those forces manifest themselves in the dialogue? Is there any particular line that jumps out at you?

3. For each character, which forces are the strongest? Which are the weakest? Does that balance ever shift? If so, when? Why?

4. If the forces shift, find the exact moment(s) that they shift. What effect does each shift have on the audience? What does the audience experience in that moment?

5. What is the new situation resulting from the shift in forces? How does it affect the script going forward? Does it change a character's relationship, his priorities, or his behavior? Does it contribute to some element of the plot?

LESSON 14: BEGINNER EXERCISE ▲

Flip through a magazine or surf the Internet to find

a photograph of two people. The people should be anonymous – no famous people or people you know. Write one to two pages of dialogue between these two people. At some point in the dialogue, have the balance of forces shift. *Try to make the shift large and noticeable.*

For Discussion:

Read the dialogues out loud to the group.

1. Have the group identify the forces acting on each character at the beginning of the script.
2. When did those forces shift? Why?
3. Can the group identify the exact moment when the forces shifted? Is there is disagreement about when it happened? If so, what caused the disagreement?
4. What effect does each shift have on the audience? What does the audience experience in that moment?
5. What is the new situation resulting from the shift in forces? How does it affect the scene going forward?

■ **LESSON 14: INTERMEDIATE AND ADVANCED EXERCISE**

Flip through a magazine or surf the Internet to find a photograph of two people. The people should be anonymous – no famous people or people you know.

FROM LINE TO LINE

Write one to two pages of dialogue between these people. At three different points in the dialogue, have the balance of forces shift. *Try to make the shifts as subtle as possible while still being clear.*

For Discussion:

1. Have the group identify the forces acting on each character at the beginning of the script.
2. When did those forces shift? Why?
3. Can the group identify the exact moments when the forces shifted? Is there is disagreement about when it happened? If so, what caused the disagreement?
4. What effect does each shift have on the audience? What does the audience experience in that moment?
5. What is the new situation resulting from each shift in forces? How does it affect the scene going forward?

LESSON 14: SOLO EXERCISE ✛

1. Write a one-page dialogue scene between two characters. Have the balance of forces between the characters shift once.
2. Rewrite the same dialogue scene. Keep it only one page in length, but have the balance of forces between the characters shift twice.

3. Rewrite the dialogue from step two. Keep it only one page in length, but have the balance of forces between the characters shift three times.

4. Rewrite the dialogue from step three. Keep it only one page in length, but have the balance of forces between the characters shift in each line.

5. Repeat this exercise as an ongoing writer's workout.

LESSON FIFTEEN:
Focusing the Scene

I n the last chapter, we talked about the shifting forces acting on dialogue. Left on their own, those forces will push and pull characters randomly. Because dialogue rides on a current of undulating forces, it is the writer's job to manipulate those forces to focus and maneuver the script. It is not enough to have a good ear for dialogue; if you can't control the forces behind the dialogue, your script will wander aimlessly. Let's imagine what this might look like. Let's say that you are writing a play. We'll call it *The Sea Gull*. Here's a scene between Arkadina, a famous actress, and Trigorin, a writer and Arkadina's lover.

TRIGORIN

Lovely day we're having.

ARKADINA

Yes, I agree. Would you like a cookie?

TRIGORIN

Yes, I'll have a cookie.

                    ARKADINA
    I think I'm going to knit a sweater.
    Maybe a blue sweater.

                    TRIGORIN
    Blue is a good color. I saw Nina this
    morning. She's a nice girl.

                    ARKADINA
    Lovely.

                    TRIGORIN
    Yes. Lovely. How's your son's new play
    coming?

                    ARKADINA
    Fine. Just fine. You know, I think
    I'm going to need blue yarn for the
    sweater.

                    TRIGORIN
    I think I saw some at a shop in town.
    Do you really want to knit? Perhaps
    you'd enjoy checkers instead.

                    ARKADINA
    I adore checkers!

You can see why an audience might get frustrated.
Scenes that wander aimlessly aren't interesting. They

don't add up to anything. It is not enough to have your dialogue move, it must move with a sense of direction. Compare my very lame scene above to an actual scene from the real play, *The Sea Gull,* written by Anton Chekhov. In this version, Arkadina and Trigorin are lovers, but Trigorin has become infatuated with Nina, a young actress. Trigorin wants to remain in town so that he can seduce Nina.

                    TRIGORIN
          Let us stay here one more day!

                    ARKADINA
          [Shakes her head.]

                    TRIGORIN
          Do let us stay!

                    ARKADINA
          I know, dearest, what keeps you here,
          but you must control yourself. Be
          sober; your emotions have intoxicated
          you a little.

                    TRIGORIN
          You must be sober, too. Be sensible;
          look upon what has happened as a true
          friend would. [Taking her hand.] You are
          capable of self-sacrifice. Be a friend
          to me and release me!

ARKADINA

[In deep excitement.] Are you so much
in love?

TRIGORIN

I am irresistibly impelled toward her.
It may be that this is just what I
need.

ARKADINA

What, the love of a country girl? Oh,
how little you know yourself!

TRIGORIN

People sometimes walk in their sleep,
and so I feel as if I were asleep, and
dreaming of her as I stand here talking to you. My imagination is shaken by
the sweetest and most glorious visions.
Release me!

ARKADINA

[Shuddering.] No, no! I am only an
ordinary woman; you must not say such
things to me. Do not torment me, Boris;
you frighten me.

TRIGORIN

You could be an extraordinary woman
if you only would. Love alone can
bring happiness on earth, love the

enchanting, the poetical love of youth,
that sweeps away the sorrows of the
world. I had no time for it when I was
young and struggling with want and lay-
ing siege to the literary fortress, but
now at last this love has come to me. I
see it beckoning; why should I fly?

ARKADINA
[With anger.] You are mad!

TRIGORIN
Release me.

ARKADINA
You have all conspired together to tor-
ture me today. [She weeps.]

TRIGORIN
[Clutching his head desperately.] She
doesn't understand me! She won't understand me!

ARKADINA
Am I then so old and ugly already that
you can talk to me like this without
any shame about another woman? [She
embraces and kisses him.] Oh, you have
lost your senses! My splendid, my glorious friend, my love for you is the
last chapter of my life. [She falls on

her knees.] You are my pride, my joy,
my light. [She embraces his knees.] I
could never endure it should you desert
me, if only for an hour; I should go
mad. Oh, my wonder, my marvel, my king!

TRIGORIN
Someone might come in. [He helps her to
rise.]

ARKADINA
Let them come! I am not ashamed of my
love. [She kisses his hands.] My jewel!
My despair! You want to do a foolish
thing, but I don't want you to do it.
I shan't let you do it! [She laughs.]
You are mine, you are mine! This fore-
head is mine, these eyes are mine, this
silky hair is mine. All your being is
mine. You are so clever, so wise, the
first of all living writers; you are
the only hope of your country. You are
so fresh, so simple, so deeply humor-
ous. You can bring out every feature
of a man or of a landscape in a single line, and your characters live and
breathe. Do you think that these words
are but the incense of flattery? Do
you think I am not speaking the truth?
Come, look into my eyes; look deep; do
you find lies there? No, you see that I

alone know how to treasure you. I alone
tell you the truth. Oh, my very dear,
you will go with me? You will? You will
not forsake me?

TRIGORIN

I have no will of my own; I never had.
I am too indolent, too submissive, too
phlegmatic, to have any. Is it possible
that women like that? Take me. Take me
away with you, but do not let me stir a
step from your side.

ARKADINA

[To herself.] Now he is mine! [Care-
lessly, as if nothing unusual had happened.] Of course you must stay here
if you really want to. I shall go, and
you can follow in a week's time. Yes,
really, why should you hurry away?

TRIGORIN

Let us go together.

ARKADINA

As you like. Let us go together then.

The second version of the scene is from one of the
most famous plays by one of the most famous playwrights of all time. The first scene is not. What is the

difference between the two scenes? At a very basic level, the second scene has focus. It has direction. Stories have a beginning and an end. Scene by scene and line by line, characters move from plot point to plot point. Chekhov was a master at steering his characters through the complicated maze of their emotional lives. As a writer, you must learn to do the same thing. If you're not able to steer the script, your dialogue will wander aimlessly. It will get lost from the story line and your audience will be bored and confused.

To take control of dialogue and steer it in a particular direction, you use the same technique that an engineer uses to move objects in a particular direction. You create a dominant force. If one force is stronger than the others, if one force dominates the others, then the character will move in the direction of that force.

In Chekhov's scene, the characters don't just say or do things willy-nilly. Arkadina does not talk about cookies. Trigorin does not chitchat about the weather. Why? Not because the characters can't do those things, only because each has something more *important* to do. Each has a dominant force that overwhelms the other forces. Trigorin wants to stay in town so that he can seduce a young actress. Arkadina is desperate to keep Trigorin with her. Those dominant forces drive the characters and their dialogue throughout the scene.

Writing teachers and textbooks tend to agree on the need for this dominant force. Different experts describe it with different names. For example, I've heard people call it "the character's goal," "the character's want," "the character's motivation," or "the character's need." All these terms are describing the same thing. I prefer the term "dominant force" because a force is defined by two characteristics: direction and magnitude

Direction

A force pushes a character in a specific direction. The key word here is "specific." Consider the following two forces acting on a character:

1. Joe wants to feel at peace with his father's suicide.
2. Joe wants to organize a rock concert to raise $500,000 to donate to charity in his father's memory.

Which force is more specific? Which force gives you a clearer sense of direction? Which tells you where the character is going to go? What he is going to do next? Which force points to specific actions that the character might undertake? Obviously, the answer is force 2. Both are powerful, but only the second force gives the character one specific direction for his actions. The dominant force for your character must have this clear sense of direction, otherwise it will be overwhelmed and disrupted by other forces in your script.

Magnitude

Magnitude refers to strength and intensity. A force may have direction, but how much energy is behind that direction? How much drive? How much motivation? To create a dominant force, a writer must not only give it direction, but she must also make it the strongest and most intense force acting upon a character. To create this strength, she must figure out where the force comes from. Does it arise from some deep internal need, such as a need to be loved, a need to feel fulfilled, or a need to be heard? Does it arise from some powerful external pressure such as a child's illness, a family's financial crisis, or a violent threat? Once you figure out the origin of the force, you can look for ways to intensify that need or pressure. What does the character lose from failure? What does he gain from success? By raising the stakes, a writer can intensify the force's power.

● LESSON 15: SCRIPT ANALYSIS EXERCISE

Have the group watch the same film or attend the same stage play. (See the Appendix for a list of suggestions.) Pick a dialogue scene from the script to review in class.

For Discussion:

1. Identify the dominant force acting upon each character in the scene.

2. For each dominant force: What is its direction? Where, specifically, is it pushing the character to go? What is it driving the character to do?

3. For each dominant force: What is its magnitude? How strong is it? What deep need or want does it come from? What happens if that need or want is not fulfilled? How might things change for the character if that need or want is fulfilled?

4. Do the dominant forces for each character come into conflict with each other? If so, where?

LESSON 15: BEGINNER EXERCISE ▲

1. Flip through a magazine or surf the Internet to find a photograph of an interesting place – it can be any place you'd like.

2. Imagine two different characters in that place. Why are they there? What is the dominant force that has brought each one to this place? What does each need to accomplish before he leaves?

3. Write a three- to five-page dialogue between those two characters set in that location. Make sure that each character's dominant force drives him through the dialogue.

For Discussion:

Review the dialogues with the group.

1. Identify the dominant force acting upon each character in the scene.
2. For each dominant force: What is its direction? Where, specifically, is it pushing the character to go? What is it driving the character to do?
3. For each dominant force: What is its magnitude? How strong is it? What deep need or want does it come from? What happens if that need or want is not fulfilled? How might things change for the character if that need or want is fulfilled?
4. Does each character maintain the dominant force throughout the dialogue? If not, where does it break? Why?
5. Do the dominant forces for each character come into conflict with each other? If so, where?

■ **LESSON 15: INTERMEDIATE AND ADVANCED EXERCISE**

1. Interview ten different people. Ask each person to name one thing that he'd like to do before he dies.
2. Look over the list of life goals. Pick one goal from the list. Imagine an original character who has this life goal. Pick a second goal from the list. Imagine a different original character who has this life goal.

3. Where might these two characters meet? In this place, how could each character pursue his life goal? What concrete action could each one take? Make this drive the dominant force for each character in the scene.

4. Write a three- to five-page dialogue between the two characters.

For Discussion:

Review the scenes with the group.

1. Identify the dominant force acting upon each character in the scene.

2. For each dominant force: What is its direction? Where, specifically, is it pushing the character to go? What is it driving the character to do?

3. For each dominant force: What is its magnitude? How strong is it? What deep need or want does it come from? What happens if that need or want is not fulfilled? How might things change for the character if that need or want is fulfilled?

4. Does each character maintain the dominant force throughout the dialogue? If not, where does it break? Why?

5. Do the dominant forces for each character come into conflict with each other? If so, where?

✛ LESSON 15: **SOLO EXERCISE**

1. Go to a public place. Find two people engaged in a conversation and observe them from a distance. Stay far enough away that you can't overhear what they are actually saying.

2. Imagine what they might be talking about. What is the dominant force that has brought each one to this place? What is it that each one needs to accomplish before he leaves?

3. Write a three- to five-page dialogue between these two characters.

4. Repeat this exercise as an ongoing writer's workout.

LESSON SIXTEEN:
Keeping Everyone in the Scene

I want you to do an experiment with a cat. If you don't own a cat, find a friend who has one. Stand at one corner of the room, far away from the animal. Now, call the cat's name. Ask the animal to walk over to you. What happens? Does the cat obey? Is she eager to be by your side? (I tried this experiment with my friend's calico. The cat glared at me, yawned, and then wandered off into the other room to give herself a tongue bath.)

Characters are like cats. They don't care about you. They aren't interested in your agenda. They will only tolerate your presence if you're offering them something they want. Retry your cat experiment with an open can of tuna in your hand. I suspect that you'll have better luck getting the animal's attention.

Every scene needs tuna. Every scene needs something that will keep all the characters in the room and keep them interested. Your characters could be doing a million other things at this moment. They could be at the gym. They could be napping. They could be reading the newspaper, having sex with a monkey, or plotting genocide. Why are they here?

They are here because, for each character, there is a dominant force that keeps her here. There is something, in this moment, that each wants *more* than working out or napping or reading the newspaper. There is something, in this moment, that is more important than everything else.

The last chapter talked about the need for a dominant force. We discussed how it gives a character focus. It points her in a particular direction. The important thing to remember is that *all* characters need focus and direction. Protagonists, antagonists, supporting characters, extras — every character needs motivation to stay in the scene. If you don't give it to them, they will wander off like cats and vomit hair balls all over your script.

Obviously, the dominant force doesn't need to be the same for each character. One person might be in the scene because he's trying to get laid while the other person is in the scene because he's trying to get a job as a night clerk. The dominant force might be anything, but it must be something that requires the character to stay in the scene. Otherwise, why would the character stay? Why would the character bother to participate? Why wouldn't she leave?

LESSON 16: **SCRIPT ANALYSIS EXERCISE** ●

Note: You can do this analysis exercise with any large, multiperson dialogue scene from an established play or screenplay. (See the Appendix for a list of suggestions.) Watch the film *His Girl Friday*. As a group, analyze the following dialogue from the climactic scene in the script:

```
INT. PRESS ROOM

Mrs. Baldwin leads a Policeman into
the room.

                    HILDY
          Mother!

                    MRS. BALDWIN
               (pointing out Burns)
          That man there!

                    HILDY
               (hugging Mrs. Baldwin)
          Mother! Oh, I'm so glad to
          see you! Are you all right?
          Tell me.

Mrs. Baldwin indignantly shakes her
off.
```

                    HARTMAN
What's the idea here?

                    POLICEMAN
This lady claims she was
kidnapped.

                    HARTMAN
What?

                    MRS. BALDWIN
They dragged me all the way
down the stairs —

                    HARTMAN
              (points to Burns)
Just a minute. Did — did
this man have anything to do
with it?

                    MRS. BALDWIN
He was the one in charge of
everything! He told them to
kidnap me!

                    BURNS
              (amazed)
Are you referring to me, Madam?

                    MRS. BALDWIN
You know you did!

                    HARTMAN
What about this, Burns? Kid-
napping, eh?

                    BURNS
Oh, trying to frame me,
eh! I never saw this woman
before in my life!

                    MRS. BALDWIN
Oh, what a thing to say! I
was standing right here —
after the girl jumped out of
the window.

                    HARTMAN
Did you get the Mayor?

                    DEPUTY
He's coming over.

                    BURNS
            (to Mrs. Baldwin)
Now, Madam — be honest. If
you were out joy riding,
drunk, and got into some
scrape, why don't you admit
it, instead of accusing
innocent people?

> MRS. BALDWIN
> You ruffian! How dare you
> say a thing like that?

> HILDY
> Please, Mother, he's just
> crazy!

> MRS. BALDWIN
> (to Sheriff)
> I'll tell you something
> more. I'll tell you why they
> did it!

> BURNS
> Come on, Sheriff. We've got
> to get bail.

> MRS. BALDWIN
> I was in here — and they had
> some kind of murderer in
> with them. They were hiding
> him!

This is a bombshell. The room is
electrified.

> HARTMAN
> Hiding him? In here?

Murphy, followed by the reporters,
comes into scene.

> MURPHY
> Hiding him where?

> HILDY
> Mother!

> REPORTERS
> Where was he?... Where'd
> they have him?... Etc.

CLOSE SHOT BURNS AT THE DESK.

> BURNS
> Madam, you're a cockeyed
> liar! And you know it!

To emphasize his righteousness, he
pounds on the desk three times, for-
getting that that is his signal to
Williams. Then, realizing what he has
done, he gasps.

MED. SHOT

Burns advances from desk, the others
retreating before him.

> BURNS
> Come on, Sheriff, we've got
> to get bail.

Three answering knocks come from the
desk.

GROUP SHOT WITH DOORWAY IN B.G.

They jump around to face the desk.

> HARTMAN
> (whispering)
> What was that?

>> REPORTERS AD LIB
> He's in the desk! — For the
> love of — He's in there!
> Etc.

> HARTMAN
> Aha! I thought so! Stand
> back, everybody!

> DEPUTY
> Look out, Sheriff. He may
> shoot!

> HARTMAN
> Get your guns out!

The policemen and deputies get out
their guns.

> HILDY
> He's harmless.

>   HARTMAN
>   Don't take any chances.
>   Shoot through the desk.

>   HILDY
>   He can't hurt anybody.
>   You've got his gun.

>   MRS. BALDWIN
>   (panic-stricken)
>   Oh, dear! Oh, dear!

>   BURNS
>   You gray-haired old Judas!

>   MRS. BALDWIN
>   Let me out! Let me out of
>   here!

She streaks for the door, flings it
open, and goes. The reporters tear out
of scene to their telephones.

>   HARTMAN
>   (to policeman)
>   You stand there!

>   MURPHY'S VOICE
>   City Desk! Quick!

> SCHWARTZ' VOICE
> Gimme the Desk!

> HARTMAN
> (to another policeman)
> You there!

> ENDICOTT'S VOICE
> City Desk! Hurry!

> MCCUE'S VOICE
> Gimme Emil...

> HARTMAN
> (pointing with gun)
> You cover the window.

> MURPHY'S VOICE
> Look out where you're point-
> ing that gun!

The Sheriff draws his men in around
the desk, their guns drawn on it.

> WILSON'S VOICE
> Lemme have the desk! Quick!

> MURPHY'S VOICE
> Hold the wire! I've got a
> flash for you!

                    BURNS
          (to Hildy)
     Call Duffy!

                    HARTMAN
     No, you don't!

                    BURNS
          (to Sheriff, furiously)
     Do you want to get us
     scooped?

                    MCCUE'S VOICE
     Emil? Hang on for a second.

                    HARTMAN
     Now then, everybody aim at
     the center. And when I say
     three —

                    HILDY
     That's murder!

                    HARTMAN
          (changing his mind)
     All right! Carl! Frank! One
     of you get on each side of
     the desk. Take hold of the
     cover.

They do.

                    HARTMAN
        Now then! We got you cov-
        ered, Williams. Don't try to
        move. Now! Everybody quiet
        and ready for an emergency.
        I'm going to count to three.

                    SCHWARTZ
        Hold it! Something coming
        up.

                    HARTMAN
        One!

                    ENDICOTT
        Hold the phone!

                    MURPHY
                (into the phone)
        I'll have it in a minute.

                    HARTMAN
        Two!

                    WILSON
                (into phone)
        Right away now!

                HARTMAN
       (turning back to desk)
   Everybody ready? All right.
   Now then, up with it.

Two deputies raise the cover. Williams
is revealed, cowering in the desk,
his hands over his face. The Sheriff
rushes on him, jabbing his gun into
him.

CLOSE SHOT SHERIFF AND WILLIAMS.

                HARTMAN
      Got you, Williams!

               WILLIAMS
    Go on — shoot me!

For Discussion:

1. List each character in this scene. What is the dominant force acting on each character? Why is each character in this room at this moment? What does he or she need to accomplish before the scene is over? Why is it important?

2. Are there forces (other than the dominant force) acting on any of the characters? If so, what are they?

3. In what way do the dominant forces draw the characters together and compel them to interact with each other?

4. Do the forces acting on each character come into conflict? If so, where?

5. Who is the one character to exit the scene? Why does she leave? What shift in forces causes the exit?

▲ **LESSON 16: BEGINNER EXERCISE**

1. Use the Yellow Pages or an Internet search to find a list of all of the businesses in your neighborhood. Select one of the businesses.

2. If possible, visit the business. Spend some time there. Get a feel for the place.

3. Brainstorm a list of people who would have a reason to be inside that business location. Who works there? Who are the customers? Who are the vendors? Who might be there by happenstance?

4. Select three people from the list. Write a three- to five-page scene between the three characters. Before you begin writing, come up with a dominant force for each character. The dominant force must be something that requires the character to remain in the scene.

For Discussion:

Review each scene with the group.

1. List each character in this scene. What is the dominant force acting on each character? Why is each character in this room at this moment? What does he or she need to accomplish before the scene is over?

2. Are there forces (other than the dominant force) acting on any of the characters? If so, what are they?

3. In what way do the dominant forces draw the characters together and compel them to interact with each other?

4. Do the forces acting on each character come into conflict? If so, where?

LESSON 16: INTERMEDIATE AND ADVANCED EXERCISE ■

1. Do steps 1 through 3 of the Beginner Exercise (above).

2. Select five people from the list. Write a five- to seven-page scene between the five characters. Before you begin writing, come up with a dominant force for each character. The dominant force must be something that requires the character to remain in the scene.

For Discussion:

1. List each character in this scene. What is the dominant force acting on each character? Why is each character in this room at this moment? What does he or she need to accomplish before the scene is over? Why is it important?

2. Are there forces (other than the dominant force) acting on any of the characters? If so, what are they?

3. In what way do the dominant forces draw the characters together and compel them to interact with each other?

4. Do the forces acting on each character come into conflict? If so, where?

✚ **LESSON 16: SOLO EXERCISE**

1. Turn on the television to a random channel. Put the sound on mute. Ignore the people on the screen, just look at the set. What does the set look like? Where is it supposed to be? What kind of feeling does it evoke?

2. Use the set as a backdrop for a completely new scene with two completely different (and original) characters. Who are the two characters? What is the dominant force that has brought them to this place? Write three to five pages of dialogue.

3. Rewrite the dialogue three times. In each rewrite, add another new character. As you add each character, come up with a dominant force that has brought the character into the scene. Make sure that each character follows his dominant force all the way through the scene.

4. Repeat this exercise as an ongoing writer's workout.

> TOM: Contradictions are what people are, bundles of contradictions, fighting them and working them out. And I refuse to be dictated to by your overly simplistic logic-chopping approach to life.
> —Mick Gordan & AC Grayling (*Grace*)

LESSON SEVENTEEN:
Maneuvering Through the Scene

It is important to remember that the dominant force is not the only force acting upon a character. It is simply the strongest force. There are other forces in the mix. These forces can have as much impact on your story as the dominant force.

If the dominant force is the engine of drama, then all of the other forces acting upon a character are the traffic. They are the forces that the character must maneuver through, detour around, or steamroll over. They will slow the character down, press her forward, bend her path, or compel her to take an unexpected turn.

The joy of watching a play or film is the joy of watching a character maneuver through the competing forces of the script. Imagine the Indy 500 with only one car on the track. Imagine a basketball game with only one player on the court. The car might move. The basketball player might score, but neither of these would be very interesting to watch.

The Indy 500 is fun because there are other cars on the road. Basketball is exciting because there are other players on the court. Just like in NASCAR or in the NBA, in the theater, audience members delight in watching characters maneuver through obstacles. As an audience, we ride along with characters on their shifting playing field. We hold our breath as characters juggle a kaleidoscope of competing forces. All of this creates exhilaration, drama, and suspense. What will happen? Which way will she go? What will he sacrifice? What will she do in the face of that problem? Which choice will he make in this difficult situation? How will they get out of this mess?

When confronted with competing forces, a character must maneuver. He might change course to accommodate both forces. He might stall out in a moment of paralysis. He might sacrifice one force in favor of another. It is this movement and change that creates the twists and bends in a plot.

The lesson for authors is this: To control your plot, do not try to control your characters. Instead, try to control the balance of forces acting on your characters. If you do this deftly, the characters will maneuver completely on their own. It's as if you are playing one of those marble-in-a-maze games: If you tilt the toy in the right direction, the marble will move where you want it to go (without you ever having to touch it).

When authors do this well, the twists and bends in the script feel natural and organic. The plot seems to move on its own. Characters' choices make sense and their problems are as real to us as our own. When authors do this badly, the twists and bends in the script feel clumsy and arbitrary. The characters' choices make no sense and their problems seem manufactured or trivial. One becomes aware of the heavy hand of the author trying to steer the script and doing it badly.

The difference between bad writing, good writing, and great writing is the degree to which authors successfully focus, juggle, weave in, and manipulate multiple forces within a script to move their characters forward through the story. Take a look at the difference between *Howard the Duck* (a bad script), *Die Hard* (a good script), and *The Godfather* (voted one of the best screenplays of all time).

Howard the Duck is a disorganized mess. Without consistent dominant forces driving the characters, the script heads off in random directions. *Die Hard*, on the other hand, is a good script. The forces underlying the action are not complicated or multifaceted, but they are clear and consistent. A few dominant forces drive the characters through the entire film. The result is a focused and hard-hitting action movie.

The difference between *Die Hard* and *The Godfather* is not the quality of the experience; it is the sophistication of the writing. While *Die Hard* surfs on a few clear dominant forces, *The Godfather* weaves a kaleidoscope of forces into its plot. There are dominant forces, but there are also a myriad of other, subtler forces acting on each character in every moment. Screenwriters Mario Puzo and Francis Ford Coppola expertly use those forces to give depth and dimension to the characters. This allows the plot to move in multiple dimensions. It is a personal story. It is a political story. It is a moral story.

● **LESSON 17: SCRIPT ANALYSIS EXERCISE**

Have the group attend the same play or watch the same movie. (See the Appendix for a list of suggestions.) Pick the most powerful or interesting dialogue scene. Review that scene with the group.

For Discussion:

1. What are the forces acting on each character at the beginning of the scene?
2. Which forces are dominant? Which are not?
3. Do the forces come into conflict? When? How?
4. How do the forces shift as a result of the conflict? Are any goals achieved? Are any desires sacrificed? Do any new wants appear?
5. Can you identify the exact moment of the shift? If so, how did you identify it?

6. What are the forces acting on each character at the end of the scene?

7. How do the forces at the end of the scene propel each character into the remainder of the story?

LESSON 17: BEGINNER EXERCISE ▲

1. Go to a clothing store or flip through a clothing catalogue. Pick out two completely different outfits. Imagine the characters who might wear them. Where are they? What is their relationship?

2. Now, while imagining the characters in that context, write down a list of at least three forces acting on each character.

3. Using that list of forces, write a three- to five-page scene between the two characters. Look for opportunities for the forces to come into conflict with each other. Look for opportunities to create shifts in the balance of forces.

For Discussion

Review each scene with the group.

1. Can you identify the three forces acting on each character?

2. Which forces are dominant? Which are not?

3. Do those forces come into conflict? When? How?

4. How do the forces shift as a result of the conflict?

Are any goals achieved? Are any desires sacrificed? Do any new wants appear?

5. Can you identify the exact moment of the shift? If so, how did you identify it?

6. Have each author discuss the process of weaving the multiple forces into the script. Was the task difficult or easy? Were some forces easier to include than others? Did the addition of multiple forces open up new dramatic opportunities or ideas?

■ LESSON 17: INTERMEDIATE AND ADVANCED EXERCISE

1. Pick any holiday (e.g., Christmas, Passover, Arbor Day). Write down a list of three characters who might be celebrating that holiday together.

2. Now, while imagining the characters in that context, write down a list of at least five forces acting on each character during the celebration.

3. Using that list of forces, write a five- to seven-page scene between the three characters. Look for opportunities for the forces to come into conflict with each other. Look for opportunities to create shifts in the balance of forces.

For Discussion:

Review each scene with the group.

1. Can you identify the five forces acting on each character?
2. Which forces are dominant? Which are not?
3. Do those forces come into conflict? When? How?
4. How do the forces shift as a result of the conflict? Are any goals achieved? Are any desires sacrificed? Do any new wants appear?
5. Can you identify the exact moment of the shift? If so, how did you identify it?
6. Have each author discuss the process of weaving the multiple forces into the script. Was the task difficult or easy? Were some forces easier to include than others? Did the addition of multiple forces open up new dramatic opportunities or ideas?

LESSON 17: SOLO EXERCISE   +

1. Brainstorm a list of forces. You can draw from your own experience, asking yourself, "What are the forces that act upon me in my own life?" You can also draw from the world of fiction and drama (What are the forces acting upon Hamlet?)
2. Write each force down on an individual index card. Begin the description of each force with the phrase "Wants to…" or "Needs to…" Try to gather

at least fifteen different forces. When describing the forces, try to keep the terms generic enough that they could apply to any character.

Here's a small sample set:

- Needs to murder an authority figure
- Wants a nap
- Wants respect
- Wants to get a puppy
- Needs a new car

3. Once you have made your index cards, draw three cards out of the hat. This will be the mix of forces acting upon Character A. Choose one to be the dominant force.

4. Draw three more cards out of the hat. This will be the mix of forces acting upon Character B. Choose one to be the dominant force.

5. Write a three- to five-page scene between Character A and Character B. Look for opportunities for the forces to come into conflict with each other. Look for opportunities to create shifts in the balance of forces.

6. As an ongoing writer's workout, keep adding to your index card file of forces and repeat this exercise on a regular basis.

ILSA: But what about us?

RICK: We'll always have Paris.
—*Casablanca* (1942)

LESSON EIGHTEEN:
Ending the Scene

Casablanca

Each character enters the scene with a dominant force – something that drives him to this place at this time. There is something that the character wants or needs and he is here, in this scene, to get it. But there are problems. There are other forces at work in the scene. These forces might come from other characters, they might come from the situation, or they might come from an internal need or drive. Wherever they come from, these forces require the character to twist and maneuver in pursuit of his goal. A king must pass a sentence of execution on a traitor, but that traitor is his beloved brother. A husband and wife must negotiate a divorce settlement, but their six-year-old daughter is playing in the same room and they do not want to upset her. A man wants to ask a coworker out on a date, but the man's boss hovers outside his office door. All of these situations create competing forces for a character to navigate.

So, you start writing a scene. You create a dominant force for each character. You make sure that there are competing forces for each character. You deftly slalom your characters through the crosscurrents of desires and goals. But how do you end the scene? When is it over?

When we talk about scenes of dialogue, we are referring to something different than film or theater scenes. In dialogue, the ending of the scene doesn't necessarily have anything to do with changing a location or time. It doesn't necessarily have anything to do with the lights going down in the theater or a blackout on the screen. It's true that these things *often* coincide with the ending of a scene, but it's not necessarily set in stone. Films are full of examples of one dialogue scene getting broken up across multiple locations or times. Even some plays will break dialogue scenes into multiple fragments of performance.

Regardless of locations, times, and blackouts, from the dialogue writer's point of view, the scene is over when one of the forces wins. When one of the many competing forces outmaneuvers or overpowers the others and accomplishes its goal for the scene, the scene is finished. A shift has occurred. A new status quo is established. The script can now move forward with a new balance of forces. These new forces will propel the characters into the remainder of the story. They will force the characters into different actions and unexplored territory.

By introducing, evolving, and then resolving the competing forces within a scene, you give the scene a basic structure: beginning, middle, and end. The scene begins as the dominant forces are introduced. It passes through its middle as the competing forces maneuver for position. It reaches its end when one force wins out over the others.

LESSON 18: SCRIPT ANALYSIS EXERCISE ●

NOTE: Beginning and intermediate writers should do this analysis exercise on a script with a traditional linear structure. The scenes should flow forward in time, one logically to the other. Advanced writers can try this analysis exercise on a script with a nontraditional or nonlinear structure. See the Appendix for a list of suggestions.

Have the group watch the same film or attend the same play. Get copies of the script. Have each member of the group review the script on her own and:

1. Mark the beginning and end of each dialogue scene.

2. At the beginning of each dialogue scene, briefly describe the forces at work in the scene.

3. At the end of each dialogue scene, make a note to describe which force has won the scene.

For Discussion:

1. Go through the script scene by scene. Is the group in agreement on where each scene begins and ends? If not, why?

2. Discuss the forces at work at the beginning and end of each dialogue scene.

   a) At the beginning: Which forces are dominant? Which are not?

   b) At the end: Which force has won the scene? How do you know? Can you point to a particular moment in the scene when the force dominated? Were any new forces added? Were any forces sacrificed?

3. How do you think the audience's perception

has shifted from the beginning of the scene to the end? Does the audience leave the scene with different knowledge, assumptions, or expectations than when it started?

LESSON 18: BEGINNER EXERCISE ▲

Write a three- to five-page scene between two characters. Use what you have learned about the introduction, competition, and resolution of forces to give your scene a beginning, a middle, and an end.

For Discussion:

Review the scenes with the group.

1. Discuss the forces at work at the beginning and end of each dialogue scene.

   At the beginning: Which forces are dominant? Which are not?

   At the end: Which force has won the scene? How do you know? Can you point to a particular moment in the scene when the force dominated? Were any new forces added? Were any forces sacrificed?

2. How do you think the audience's perception has shifted from the beginning of the scene to the end? Does the audience leave the scene with different knowledge, assumptions, or expectations than when it started?

3. Look at the middle of the scene. When and where did conflicting forces cause twists and bends in the plot of the scene?

4. If you were an audience member, in what way(s) would you identify with the forces acting on each character? What feelings would the scene provoke?

■ **LESSON 18: INTERMEDIATE AND ADVANCED EXERCISE**

Write a five- to seven-page scene between four characters. Use what you have learned about the introduction, competition, and resolution of forces to give your scene a beginning, a middle, and an end.

For Discussion:

1. Discuss the forces at work at the beginning and end of each dialogue scene.

a) At the beginning: Which forces are dominant? Which are not?

b) At the end: Which force has won the scene? How do you know? Can you point to a particular moment in the scene when the force dominated? Were any new forces added? Were any forces sacrificed?

2. How do you think the audience's perception has shifted from the beginning of the scene to

the end? Does the audience leave the scene with different knowledge, assumptions, or expectations than when it started?

3. Look at the middle of the scene. When and where did conflicting forces cause twists and bends in the plot of the scene?

4. If you were an audience member, in what way(s) would you identify with the forces acting on each character? What feelings would the scene provoke?

LESSON 18: SOLO EXERCISE   +

1. Create two original characters. Imagine them at the beginning of a scene. Who are they? Where are they? What are they doing? What are the dominant forces acting on each character? What are the smaller forces acting on them?

2. Write down three adjectives to describe each character at the beginning of the scene. The adjectives might describe the character's state of mind, his beliefs, or his relationship to the other. Here's an example.

Bob and Sally at a Hot Dog Stand: Beginning of the Scene

Bob: Agitated, Jealous, and Hungry

Sally: Vain, Perky, and In Love with Bob

3. Look at your list of adjectives. For each adjective, list its opposite. This will be the state of things at the end of your scene.

Bob and Sally at a Hot Dog Stand: End of the Scene

Bob: Calm, Disinterested, and Sated

Sally: Humbled, Morose, and Loathing Bob

4. Write a three- to five-page scene between the two characters. Begin with the characters in the state described with the beginning adjectives. By the end of the scene, the characters should be in the state described by the ending adjectives. Use what you have learned about manipulating the forces within the script to steer the characters through the scene and to wrap it up at the end.

5. Repeat this exercise as an ongoing writer's workout.

LESSON NINETEEN:
Rewriting the Scene

O nce you have mastered the techniques in this book, you can use them to identify problems in your dialogue and to rewrite an existing scene. Building upon what you have learned, this chapter takes you through a set of focused rewrite exercises.

LESSON 19: REWRITE EXERCISE: IN THE AUDIENCE'S SHOES

Select a scene you wish to rewrite. This might be a scene from an exercise, a script-in-development, or a completed full-length work.

1. Put the scene away for at least one week.
2. Look at the scene with fresh eyes. Reread the scene or, if you are part of a writing group, review the scene with the group.
3. Imagine that you are an audience member watching this scene.
4. What are you focused on in this scene? What is the most gripping or engaging aspect of the scene?

5. With what or with whom do you empathize? With what issues or people do you identify?
6. What is the world like in this scene? How do you feel in this world?
7. What twists or revelations in the scene are surprising or unexpected?
8. As an audience member, how has your perception shifted from the beginning of the scene to the end? Do you leave the scene with different knowledge, assumptions, or expectations than when it started?
9. Look through the rewrite exercises below. Based on your observations, would your scene benefit from any of these exercises? If so, do them.
10. Once you have completed the selected rewrite exercises below, repeat steps 1 through 9 of this exercise.

LESSON 19: REWRITE EXERCISE: VOICES

1. Read your scene all the way through.
2. Make a list of the character voices that you want to rewrite.
3. Pick one of the characters from your list. Go through the scene and focus exclusively on that character.
   a) Read sections of dialogue out loud. Do the punctuation and phrasing of the dialogue

effectively capture the rhythm and flavor of the character's speech? Rewrite as needed.

   b) Line by line, identify the tones of the character's voice. Does the character's speech include multiple tones? Do those tones accurately reflect the character's background, his environment, and the forces acting upon him? Are there tones that should be added? Are there tones that should be removed? Rewrite as needed.

4. Repeat step 3 for each character on your list.

LESSON 19: REWRITE EXERCISE: INTERACTIONS

1. Read your scene all the way through.

2. Pick a relationship in the scene to focus on. For example, if your scene contains three characters – Bob, Sue, and Helen – decide whether you want to focus on the relationship between Bob and Sue, Bob and Helen, or Sue and Helen.

3. Go through the scene and focus exclusively on that one relationship.

4. What is the status relationship between the two characters? In their interactions, do they both try to take high status? Do they both try to take low status? Does one take high and one take low? In the course of the scene, do they ever change their status goals/roles? If so, when?

Why? Review the scene line by line and tweak the dialogue to accurately reflect each character's status role (in relation to the other) moment to moment through the scene.

5. Return to step 2 and select a different relationship in the scene. Repeat steps 2 through 4 until you have covered all of the relationships within the scene.

LESSON 19: REWRITE EXERCISE: THE WORLD

1. Read your scene all the way through.
2. As succinctly and clearly as possible, give a name to the world in which this scene takes place.
3. Identify the larger worlds that this world is a part of. Identify the smaller worlds contained within this world.
4. Select one world from the list of worlds that you have described. Focus exclusively on that world and its role within the scene.
5. Describe the setting and situation of this world. What does it look like when you walk around it? What does it sound like? How does it feel? Does the dialogue reflect this environment? If not, rewrite as needed.
6. What defines status in this world? To what people and values does the world assign high status? To what people and values does the world assign

low status? Does the dialogue reflect these status expectations? If not, rewrite as needed.

7. What are the status tools and rituals in this world? Does the dialogue reflect the use of those tools and rituals? If not, rewrite as needed.

8. Make a list of each character in the scene. Pick a particular character to focus on.

9. How does this character fit into this world? Does the world attempt to give him high status or low status? How does the character feel about that status role? Are the character's status role within the world and his feelings about it reflected in the character's dialogue? If not, rewrite as needed.

10. Repeat steps 8 and 9 for each character in the scene.

11. Repeat steps 4 through 10 for each world on your list.

LESSON 19: REWRITE EXERCISE: FORCES AT WORK

1. Read your scene all the way through.

2. List each character in this scene.

3. What is the dominant force acting on each character? Why is each character in this room at this moment? What does he or she need to accomplish before the scene is over? Make sure that

each character has a dominant force keeping him in the scene. If he does not, rewrite as needed.

4. For each dominant force: What is its direction? Where, specifically, is it pushing the character to go? What is it driving the character to do? If you cannot answer this question clearly and succinctly, rewrite the dialogue to make it clear.

5. For each dominant force: What is its magnitude? How strong is it? What deep need or want does it come from? What happens if that need or want is not fulfilled? How might things change for the character if that need or want is fulfilled? If the answers to these questions are not clear, rewrite as needed.

6. Are there forces (other than the dominant force) acting on any of the characters? If so, what are they? Does the dialogue reflect all of the forces acting upon each character? If not, rewrite as needed.

LESSON 19: REWRITE EXERCISE: TURNING POINTS

1. Review the middle of the scene. In what way do the forces draw the characters together and compel them to interact with each other? If a character does not have a force drawing him into the action of the scene, rewrite to give him one.

2. Do the forces acting on each character come into conflict? If so, where? If not, look at each combination of forces and find opportunities to bring them into conflict. Rewrite as needed.

3. Go through the scene and mark any moments where the balance of forces shifts. Can you find the exact moments? Can you articulate exactly what has shifted? If not, rewrite to make the shifts clear.

4. Go through the scene and look for additional opportunities to shift the balance of forces. Have you missed an interesting twist or undercurrent? If so, rewrite as needed.

LESSON 19: REWRITE EXERCISE: THE ENDING

1. Review the end of the scene. Which force has won? How do you know? Can you point to a particular moment in the scene when the force dominated? If the answers to any of these questions are unclear, rewrite as needed to make them clear.

2. How has the balance of forces changed from the beginning of the scene to the end? How is the new status quo different than the old one? If the answer to this question is unclear, rewrite as needed to make it clear.

LESSON TWENTY:
Scene to Script

Sunday in the Park with George

Once you have mastered the fundamentals of dialogue and can maneuver that dialogue deftly
through a scene, you are ready to proceed to a full
script. Organizing the plot of a full-length script exceeds
the scope of this book. (For a list of suggested reading
on this topic, see the Appendix.) The task of writing a

full-length script goes far beyond mere dialogue and scene construction; however there are core principles from this book that you can expand and apply to a full-length work.

The Dominant Force (The Beginning)

As discussed in a previous chapter, plays and films (like all of the performing arts) are experienced over a period of time. They are not instant events. They last. They travel from beginning to end. They move. The fundamental job of a scriptwriter is to create the series of changes that move the audience through the performance.

It's a big job. So how do we do it? How do we create moments of change? Somewhere, thousands and thousands of years ago, the first dramatic writer faced this problem. The answer that she came up with is the answer that most writers still use to this day: We get other people to make these changes for us. We call them characters.

Within the world of plays and films, characters are very good at changing things. Sure, there are other things a writer could put in his script that would, without the help of any characters, cause things to change – lightning could strike, for example, or a wild animal could go on a rampage – but those things aren't very reliable. It's hard to build a two-hour sequence of changes around them. People are much better at changing things. Unlike lightning, people have free will. Unlike wild animals, people have large, intelligent brains. If you want to make something happen on stage or film, the easiest way to do it is to put some people up there. (Some writers find other ways to do it: They create a world in which lightning has free will or wild animals are capable of intelligent thought, but the ultimate effect is still the same: Things start changing.)

So, you create a world, you fill it with characters, and the characters run around and start changing things. They say stuff, they do stuff, they move around. Suddenly the world is filled with activity. All sorts of characters are changing things all the time. You've solved the problem of nothing happening, but you've created a new problem: Everything is happening, all the time, and in no particular order. You've got changes happening in all sorts of directions and the audience doesn't know which ones to follow. Let's imagine what this might look like. We're writing a script. We'll call it *Hamlet*.

> **Change 1:** Hamlet's father's ghost appears. He tells Hamlet that he was murdered by his brother. He begs Hamlet to avenge his death.
>
> **Change 2:** Hamlet goes to the salon and gets a facial.

Change 3: Rosencrantz and Guildenstern open a dog training facility outside of the castle.

Change 4: Ophelia and Hamlet's mother bake cookies for the court.

Change 5: Hamlet's uncle kills himself.

Change 6: Ophelia decides to take up basket weaving.

Change 7: Rosencrantz asks Ophelia to marry him.

Change 8: Hamlet's mother goes into Freudian psychoanalysis.

Change 9: Hamlet tries to murder Ophelia.

Change 10: A group of players arrives at court. They do a production of *Seven Brides for Seven Brothers*.

Change 11: Guildenstern decides to buy an Italian villa.

Change 12: Polonius writes a self-help book.

You can see why an audience would eventually get frustrated.

What we need is a way to organize things. Thousands of years ago, dramatic writers stumbled on two organizing principles that still work to this day:

Focus on One Central Character

Rather than trying to follow what everyone in this entire made-up world is doing, have the audience just follow one character. We'll call him the "Main Character" or the "Central Character." Let's just follow Hamlet, for example.

> **Change 1:** Hamlet's father's ghost appears. He tells Hamlet that he was murdered by his brother. He begs Hamlet to avenge his death.
>
> **Change 2:** Hamlet goes to the salon and gets a facial.
>
> **Change 3:** Hamlet goes to a bar and gets drunk.
>
> **Change 4:** Hamlet decides to take a fencing lesson.
>
> **Change 5:** Hamlet polishes his shoes.
>
> **Change 6:** Hamlet takes his mother out to lunch.
>
> **Change 7:** Hamlet goes riding with his friends, Rosencrantz and Guildenstern.

And so on. So, this is a little better. At least we're following the same person. We're not completely confused any more. We're just bored. We don't care about what Hamlet is doing. The whole thing doesn't seem to add up to anything. What we need is another organizing principle.

Give the Central Character a Dominant Force

If the central character has a dominant force, he's not going to just initiate random changes in this world. He's not going to just wander around doing stuff. He's going to try to change things in a particular direction. He will initiate changes in pursuit of a goal. Let's give Hamlet a goal:

> **Change 1:** Hamlet's father's ghost appears. He tells Hamlet that he was murdered by his brother. He begs Hamlet to avenge his death.

So, Hamlet's goal is to take vengeance for his father's death by murdering the king. That leads to...

> **Change 2:** Hamlet makes the guards, who were witnesses to the ghost's appearance, swear an oath of secrecy.

> **Change 3:** Hamlet begins to behave erratically. This behavior confuses the king and queen. Everyone at court tries to figure out what is wrong with Hamlet.

> **Change 4:** A group of actors comes to court. Hamlet writes a play for them to perform. The play imitates the king's murder of his father. Hamlet hopes to see evidence of the

king's guilt in his reaction to the play.

Change 5: The king is horrified by the play. Hamlet realizes that the king is truly guilty.

Change 6: Hamlet goes to kill the king, but he finds the king praying. Hamlet is determined that the king should die in a state of sin, so he does not kill him.

And so on. Now that Hamlet has a dominant force, he doesn't just change things willy-nilly. Every change he makes on stage is in pursuit of a goal. Hamlet doesn't get a facial; he doesn't polish his shoes; he doesn't take his mother out to lunch. Why? Not because he can't do those things, but because they are not part of his agenda.

The audience now has a clear set of stepping-stones that lead in a particular direction. Out of these changes, the audience can assemble a narrative. They keep leaping onto new stones because they want to find out what happens next. They want to see where the changes will lead them.

The dominant force is a powerful tool for focusing a story, setting it in motion, and giving it direction. Because it is so powerful, 99% of all successful plays and screenplays introduce one somewhere within the first quarter of the story. It is, in effect, the story's beginning.

Competing Forces (The Middle)

The dominant force is not the only force in the script. There are other forces at work. Why? Because if there weren't, you'd have some very short scripts.

Imagine you're writing *Macbeth*. The dominant force for Macbeth is that he wants to become king. Without any other forces in the script, the existing king (and his subjects) would just hand over the crown. No fight, no argument, no debate, they'd just give it to him. Macbeth wants it in Scene 1. He gets it in Scene 2. Play over – go home.

In *Raiders of the Lost Ark*, Indiana Jones wants to find the Lost Ark of the Covenant. Without other forces in the script, he'd simply fly to Egypt, dig it up, and bring it back to the U.S. Ten minutes – movie over. And you haven't even started your popcorn yet.

As the writer, you've got to do better than this. People are paying good money to see your work and if it's over in scene two, they're going to want their money back. So, you've got to find a way to make your story last a while.

To do this, you must create competing forces within your script. The dominant force (the goal) is not the only force. Other forces will cause twists, bends, and setbacks in your character's path. The ways in which your character wrestles with these forces will give your story a middle. They will create obstacles that lengthen the distance between beginning and end.

The most obvious of these forces will be external. They will come from other characters within the script. Writing textbooks tend to call these characters "antagonists" or "opposition characters." The Nazis fight against Indiana Jones for the Ark. Claudius plots against Hamlet. Duncan leads an army against Macbeth.

Competing forces can also come from the natural world. Consider the sinking ship in the movie *Titanic*. It's not a person, but it certainly causes twists, bends, and setbacks in the heroes' efforts to get to safety.

Less obvious, but just as important, are the competing forces that come from within the character himself. Indiana Jones must deal with the external force of the Nazis, but at the same time, Jones has competing internal needs. He wants to save the ark, but he also wants to be loyal to his friends and to protect his girlfriend. Some of the most entertaining twists and turns in the script come when Jones must juggle the competing forces within his own self.

Hamlet sets out to kill his uncle, but struggles with his own internal competing forces. He must overcome fears about the fate of his soul. He feels some obligation to his girlfriend. He longs for the closeness of his mother. Some part of him questions the validity of his goal. Indeed, the first half of *Hamlet* can be read as Hamlet freeing himself from these conflicting forces. One by one, scene by scene, he cuts the internal strings that are holding back the dominant force of vengeance.

Victory of One Force over the Others (The End)

A person with a dominant force is a character. A person pursuing that dominant force in the face of other competing forces is a plot. But when is the plot over?

A plot is over when it resolves — when one of the forces permanently triumphs over the others. This triumph removes the tension of conflicting forces and creates a new status quo.

In concrete terms, this means that either 1) the central character gets her goal and the character's dominant force wins; or 2) the central character permanently gives up her goal and the character's dominant force loses.

The central character gets her goal: Hamlet kills the king. Sauron's ring falls into the fires of Mount Doom. Viola marries Orsino. In *Hamlet*, *Lord of the Rings*, and *Twelfth Night*, the plot resolves with the main character achieving his or her goal. In the course of achieving this goal, he has had to conquer, sacrifice, or tame all of the other, conflicting forces in the script.

The central character permanently gives up her goal: Blanche DuBois gets carted off to a mental hospital. Rick tells Ilsa to get on the plane. Macbeth gets killed by Duncan. Oedipus gets sent into exile. In *Streetcar Named Desire*, *Casablanca*, *Macbeth*, and *Oedipus Rex*, the plot resolves when the main character permanently gives up his or her goal.

The character's dominant force has tried every tactic, but in the end, it is beaten by one of the other competing forces in the script. Blanche's psyche is beaten down by Stanley. Rick sacrifices his and Ilsa's love for larger, nobler purposes. Macbeth is killed by Duncan. Oedipus is sent into exile.

The important thing about all of these scenarios is that the question of whether the main character will achieve his goal is resolved in a permanent way. The audience anticipates no more changes in pursuit of this particular goal. The king is dead. Sauron's ring is destroyed. Viola is married. These things are permanent. There is no coming back from the mental hospital for Blanche. There is no return from the grave for Macbeth. Rick and Ilsa will never see each other again and Oedipus will never regain his kingdom. The tension between all of the competing forces is resolved. The pursuit of the goal is finished, therefore the story is over.

LESSON 20: SCRIPT ANALYSIS EXERCISE ●

As a group, watch the same film or attend the same stage play. (See the Appendix for a list of suggestions.)

For Discussion:

1. Identify the central characters.
2. For each character, what is the dominant force acting upon him?
3. What is the direction of that dominant force? What does it drive the character to do or achieve?
4. What is the magnitude of that dominant force? Why is the character driven by this force? What is at stake for the character?
5. When is the dominant force introduced?
6. Once it is introduced, does the dominant force continue through the entire story?
7. In what ways does each character's dominant force come into conflict?
8. Over the course of the script, what are the other forces acting upon each character? How strong are they relative to the dominant force?
9. In what ways do those come into conflict?
10. What twists and bends in the plot are a result of this conflict?
11. How does the story resolve? Which force emerges as victorious over the others?
12. How have things changed between the beginning of the story and the end?

LESSON 20: **BEGINNER EXERCISE**　▲

Using the following questions, create a two- to four-page brainstorming outline for a short script.

1. The setting: Describe the world of this script.
2. Identify two or three central characters. Who are they? What is their situation?
3. What is the dominant force for each character?
4. What are the other forces acting on each character?
5. What are three different situations in which those forces might come into conflict? What will each character do to maneuver through the conflict? How will the characters be forced to change as a result of each conflict?
6. How will the conflict between the forces resolve? Which force will win?
7. How will the characters and their situation be permanently changed as a result?

For Discussion:

Review the brainstorming outlines with the group.

1. What aspects of the outline interest you the most? What are you most emotionally engaged by?
2. What feeling do you get about the experience of this script? What is the overall tone? Funny? Sad? Epic?

3. What aspects of the outline are clear? What aspects of the outline are not clear? Ask the writer to fill in the gaps.

■ LESSON 20: INTERMEDIATE AND ADVANCED EXERCISE

Using the following questions, create an eight- to twelve-page brainstorming outline for a full-length script.

1. The setting: Describe the world of this script.
2. Identify three to five central characters. Who are they? What is their situation?
3. What is the dominant force for each character?
4. What are the other forces acting on each character?
5. What are five different situations in which those forces might come into conflict? What will each character do to maneuver through the conflict? How will the characters be forced to change as a result of each conflict?
6. How will the conflict between the forces resolve? Which force will win?
7. How will the characters and their situation be permanently changed as a result?

For Discussion:

Review the brainstorming outlines with the group.

1. What aspects of the outline interest you the most? What are you most emotionally engaged by?

2. What feeling do you get about the experience of this script? What is the overall tone? Funny? Sad? Epic?

3. What aspects of the outline are clear? What aspects of the outline are not clear? Ask the writer to fill in the gaps.

LESSON 20: SOLO EXERCISE ✚

1. Do the Beginner Exercise (above).

2. Use the notes to write a short play or short screenplay (ten to twenty pages). Make sure that the script has a clear beginning, middle, and end. Use the Rewrite Exercises in Lesson 19 to polish the script.

3. When your script is completed, find a competition or a festival of short scripts and submit it.

4. Do this exercise two to three times per year as a regular writer's workout.

OBI-WAN KENOBI: The Force will be with you.
Always.
—*Star Wars* (1977)

Conclusion

Now that you've read all the lessons and done all the exercises, it's time to put the book away. The whole purpose of this book is to get you to the point where you no longer need it. The goal is to internalize the lessons so that they become instinctive. A professional piano player does not need to remind himself consciously of proper fingering techniques every time he plays a piece of music. In the same way, professional scriptwriters do not need to remind themselves consciously of the mechanics of dialogue.

The truth? Scriptwriters don't actually think about all this stuff every time they write. Writing theory is like music theory. It's there to guide you while you're learning, support you as you become proficient, and provide you something to fall back on when you have a problem. If you allow theory and technique to take over your entire writing process, it will only get in your way. So put the book down. Forget about the lessons and just write. If you hit a wall or have a problem, then dig out the book, dust it off, and review some of its fundamental principles:

- The most interesting character voices blend together a mix of tones (Lessons 1–3).
- All human interactions are status interactions (Lessons 4–10).
- The world of your script has as much effect on dialogue as the characters in your script (Lesson 11).
- You must know who your characters are before you will know how they speak (Lesson 12).
- A line of dialogue reflects the sum of all forces acting upon a character. To steer the dialogue you must steer the underlying forces of the script (Lessons 13–20).

So, good-bye for now. Tuck this book away on a high shelf. Let it sit unopened and untouched… until you need it again.

APPENDIX

Script Analysis Suggestions

This is a list of suggestions for scripts to analyze using the Script Analysis Exercise in each lesson. Keep in mind that the Script Analysis Exercises and Discussion Questions can be applied to any script you choose to bring in.

Lessons 1–3

Film / Television	Theater
Annie Hall (1977)	*The Duck Variations* by David Mamet
Boogie Nights (1997)	*Three Sisters* by Anton Chekhov
Pride and Prejudice (TV: BBC, 1995): episodes 1 and 2	*Angels in America* by Tony Kushner
	Ma Rainey's Black Bottom by August Wilson
American Beauty (1999)	*Thom Pain (Based on Nothing)* by Will Eno
Apocalypse Now (1979)	*Long Day's Journey Into Night* by Eugene O'Neill
Reality Bites (1994)	*Frankie and Johnny in the Clair de Lune* by
Toy Story (1995)	Terrence McNally
Goodfellas (1990)	*God's Ear* by Jenny Schwartz
Swingers (1996)	*Man and Superman* by George Bernard Shaw
The Dark Knight (2008)	*Balm in Gilead* by Lanford Wilson

Lesson 4

Film / Television	Theater
Brighton Beach Memoirs (1986)	*The Odd Couple* by Neil Simon
Biloxi Blues (1988)	*The Last of the Red Hot Lovers* by Neil Simon
The Out of Towners (1970)	*Barefoot in the Park* by Neil Simon

Lessons 5–9

Film / Television	Theater
A Fish Called Wanda (1988)	*Death of a Salesman* by Arthur Miller
All About Eve (1950)	*Blithe Spirit* by Noel Coward
Amadeus (1984)	*The Little Foxes* by Lillian Hellman
Midnight Run (1988)	*Macbeth* by William Shakespeare
The Graduate (1967)	*Pygmalion* by George Bernard Shaw
Fraiser (TV: 1993–2004)	*The Story* by Tracy Scott Wilson
The Sopranos (TV: 1999–2007)	*True West* by Sam Shepard
The Hunt for Red October (1990)	*The Importance of Being Earnest* by Oscar Wilde
The Producers (1968)	*Intimate Apparel* by Lynn Nottage
The West Wing (TV: 1999–2006)	*Noises Off* by Michael Fryan
Jerry Maguire (1996)	*Art* by Yasmina Reza
Ratatouille (2007)	*Steel Magnolias* by Robert Harling
On the Waterfront (1954)	*Medea* by Euripides
Frost/Nixon (2008)	*The Real Thing* by Tom Stoppard
Little Miss Sunshine (2006)	*A Flea in Her Ear* by Georges Feydeau

Lesson 10

Film / Television	Theater
Midnight Cowboy (1969)	*Doubt* by John Patrick Shanley
Witness (1985)	*Glengarry Glen Ross* by David Mamet
The Wire (TV: 2002–2008)	*Animal Farm* by George Orwell and Peter Hall

Lesson 11

Film / Television	Theater
The Princess Bride (1987)	*A Midsummer Night's Dream* by William
Being John Malkovich (1999)	Shakespeare
Fargo (1996)	*The Glass Menagerie* by Tennessee Williams
Star Wars (1977)	*Blasted* by Sarah Kane
Steel Magnolias (1989)	*Marisol* by José Rivera

Lesson 16

Film / Television	Theater
His Girl Friday (1940)	*August: Osage County* by Tracy Letts
Some Like it Hot (1959)	*Hay Fever* by Noel Coward

Lesson 18

Film / Television: Beginner and Intermediate	Theater: Beginner and Intermediate
The Silence of the Lambs (1991)	*The Philadelphia Story* by Philip Barry
Raiders of the Lost Ark (1981)	*Dividing the Estate* by Horton Foote
Gone with the Wind (1939)	*Wait Until Dark* by Frederick Knott
The Sting (1973)	*The Wild Duck* by Henrik Ibsen
Film / Television: Advanced	Theater: Advanced
Pulp Fiction (1994)	*Betrayal* by Harold Pinter
Memento (2000)	*Arcadia* by Tom Stoppard
Groundhog Day (1993)	*Mnemonic* by Theatre de Complicite
Eternal Sunshine of the Spotless Mind (2004)	*now then again* by Penny Penniston
Citizen Kane (1941)	*Waiting for Godot* by Samuel Beckett

Lessons 12-15; 17; 20

Film / Television	Theater
The Godfather (1972)	*Miss Julie* by August Strindberg
Die Hard (1988)	*Boy Gets Girl* by Rebecca Gilman
Thelma & Louise (1991)	*Hedda Gabler* by Henrik Ibsen
The Untouchables (1987)	*The Clean House* by Sarah Ruhl
Chinatown (1974)	*A Streetcar Named Desire* by Tennessee Williams
One Flew Over the Cuckoo's Nest (1975)	*The Goat, or Who Is Sylvia?* by Edward Albee
Back to the Future (1985)	*The Pillowman* by Martin McDonagh
Casablanca (1942)	*Fences* by August Wilson
Shakespeare in Love (1998)	*The House of Yes* by Wendy MacLeod
Tootsie (1982)	*A Flea in Her Ear* by Georges Feydeau
Schindler's List (1993)	*Henry V* by William Shakespeare
Broadcast News (1987)	*The Promise* by José Rivera
The Bridge on the River Kwai (1957)	*Fuddy Meers* by David Lindsay-Abaire
Psycho (1960)	*Proof* by David Auburn
When Harry Met Sally (1989)	*Who's Afraid of Virginia Woolf* by Edward Albee
Wall-E (2008)	*Hamlet* by William Shakespeare
The Shawshank Redemption (1994)	*The Good Person of Szechwan* by Bertolt Brecht

Course and Workshop Syllabus Suggestions

BEGINNER

Course and Workshop Suggestions	1-Day Workshop	2-Day Workshop	5-Day Workshop	10-Week Class	15-Week Class
1. Capturing the Voice	Day 1	Day 1	Day 1	Week 1	Week 1
1. Script Analysis Exercise	Day 1	Day 1	Day 1	Week 1	Week 1
1. Beginner Exercise	Day 1	Day 1	Day 1		Week 1
1. Intermediate and Advanced Exercise					
1. Solo Exercise					
2. Imitating a Voice	Day 1	Day 1	Day 1	Week 1	Week 2
2. Script Analysis Exercise	Day 1	Day 1	Day 1		Week 2
2. Beginner Exercise	Day 1	Day 1	Day 1	Week 1	Week 2
2. Intermediate and Advanced Exercise					
2. Solo Exercise					
3. Creating an Original Voice	Day 1	Day 1	Day 1	Week 1	Week 3
3. Script Analysis Exercise	Day 1	Day 1	Day 1	Week 1	Week 3
3. Beginner Exercise	Day 1	Day 1	Day 1	Week 2	Week 3
3. Intermediate and Advanced Exercise					
3. Solo Exercise					
4. Status		Day 2	Day 2	Week 2	Week 4
4. Script Analysis Exercise					
4. Beginner Exercise					Week 4
4. Intermediate and Advanced Exercise					
4. Solo Exercise					
5. Give and Take		Day 2	Day 2	Week 2	Week 4
5. Script Analysis Exercise				Week 2	Week 4
5. Beginner Exercise		Day 2	Day 2	Week 2	Week 4
5. Intermediate and Advanced Exercise					
5. Solo Exercise					
6. Building Dialogue		Day 2	Day 2	Week 2	Week 5
6. Script Analysis Exercise					
6. Beginner Exercise		Day 2	Day 2	Week 3	Week 5
6. Intermediate and Advanced Exercise					
6. Solo Exercise					
7. Dialogue on Shifting Sands		Day 2	Day 2	Week 3	Week 5

BEGINNER

Course and Workshop Suggestions	1-Day Workshop	2-Day Workshop	5-Day Workshop	10-Week Class	15-Week Class
7. Script Analysis Exercise		Day 2	Day 2	Week 3	Week 5
7. Beginner Exercise		Day 2	Day 2	Week 4	Week 6
7. Intermediate and Advanced Exercise					
7. Solo Exercise					
8. Strengths and Weaknesses			Day 3	Week 4	Week 6
8. Script Analysis Exercise			Day 3	Week 4	Week 6
8. Beginner Exercise			Day 3	Week 5	Week 6
8. Intermediate and Advanced Exercise					
8. Solo Exercise					
9. Friends and Foes			Day 3	Week 5	Week 7
9. Script Analysis Exercise			Day 3	Week 5	Week 7
9. Beginner Exercise			Day 3	Week 6	Week 7
9. Intermediate and Advanced Exercise					
9. Solo Exercise					
10. Tools			Day 3	Week 6	Week 8
10. Script Analysis Exercise			Day 3	Week 6	Week 8
10. Beginner Exercise			Day 3	Week 7	Week 8
10. Intermediate and Advanced Exercise					
10. Solo Exercise					
11. Setting the Scene					
11. Script Analysis Exercise					
11. Beginner Exercise					
11. Intermediate and Advanced Exercise					
11. Solo Exercise					
12. Populating the Scene					
12. Introduction					
12. Script Analysis Exercise					
12. Beginner Exercise					
12. Intermediate and Advanced Exercise					
12. Solo Exercise					
13. Crafting the Line			Day 4	Week 7	Week 9
13. Script Analysis Exercise			Day 4	Week 7	Week 9
13. Beginner Exercise					
13. Intermediate and Advanced Exercise					
13. Solo Exercise					
14. From Line to Line			Day 4	Week 7	Week 9
14. Script Analysis Exercise			Day 4	Week 7	Week 9
14. Beginner Exercise			Day 4	Week 8	Week 10

BEGINNER

Course and Workshop Suggestions	1-Day Workshop	2-Day Workshop	5-Day Workshop	10-Week Class	15-Week Class
14. Intermediate and Advanced Exercise					
14. Solo Exercise					
15. Focusing the Scene			Day 4	Week 8	Week L
15. Script Analysis Exercise			Day 4	Week 8	Week I
15. Beginner Exercise			Day 4	Week 9	Week I
15. Intermediate and Advanced Exercise					
15. Solo Exercise					
16. Keeping Everyone in the Scene			Day 5		
16. Script Analysis Exercise					
16. Beginner Exercise					
16. Intermediate and Advanced Exercise					
16. Solo Exercise					
17. Maneuvering Through the Scene			Day 5	Week 9	Week I
17. Script Analysis Exercise			Day 5	Week 9	Week I
17. Beginner Exercise			Day 5	Week 9	Week I
17. Intermediate and Advanced Exercise					
17. Solo Exercise					
18. Ending the Scene			Day 5	Week 9	Week I
18. Script Analysis Exercise			Day 5		Week I
18. Beginner Exercise			Day 5	Week 10	Week I
18. Intermediate and Advanced Exercise					
18. Solo Exercise					
19. Rewriting the Scene					Week I
19. In the Audience's Shoes					Week I
19. Voices					Week I
19. Interactions					Week I
19. The World					Week I
19. Forces at Work					Week I
19. Turning Points					Week I
19. The Ending					Week I
20. Scene to Script				Week 10	Week I
20. Script Analysis Exercise				Week 10	Week I
20. Beginner Exercise					Week I
20. Intermediate and Advanced Exercise					
20. Solo Exercise					

INTERMEDIATE

Course and Workshop Suggestions	1-Day Workshop	2-Day Workshop	5-Day Workshop	10-Week Class	15-Week Class
1. Capturing the Voice					
1. Script Analysis Exercise					
1. Beginner Exercise					
1. Intermediate and Advanced Exercise					
1. Solo Exercise					
2. Imitating a Voice					
2. Script Analysis Exercise					
2. Beginner Exercise					
2. Intermediate and Advanced Exercise					
2. Solo Exercise					
3. Creating an Original Voice	Day 1	Day 1	Day 1	Week 1	Week 1
3. Script Analysis Exercise				Week 1	Week 1
3. Beginner Exercise					
3. Intermediate and Advanced Exercise	Day 1	Day 1	Day 1	Week 1	Week 1
3. Solo Exercise					
4. Status	Day 1	Day 1	Day 1	Week 2	Week 2
4. Script Analysis Exercise					
4. Beginner Exercise					
4. Intermediate and Advanced Exercise					
4. Solo Exercise					
5. Give and Take	Day 1	Day 1	Day 1	Week 2	Week 2
5. Script Analysis Exercise				Week 2	Week 2
5. Beginner Exercise					
5. Intermediate and Advanced Exercise				Week 2	Week 2
5. Solo Exercise					
6. Building Dialogue	Day 1	Day 1	Day 1	Week 2	Week 2
6. Script Analysis Exercise					
6. Beginner Exercise					
6. Intermediate and Advanced Exercise	Day 1	Day 1	Day 1	Week 3	Week 3
6. Solo Exercise					
7. Dialogue on Shifting Sands	Day 1	Day 1	Day 1	Week 3	Week 3
7. Script Analysis Exercise	Day 1	Day 1	Day 1	Week 3	Week 3
7. Beginner Exercise					
7. Intermediate and Advanced Exercise	Day 1	Day 1	Day 1	Week 4	Week 4
7. Solo Exercise					

INTERMEDIATE

Course and Workshop Suggestions	1-Day Workshop	2-Day Workshop	5-Day Workshop	10-Week Class	15-Week Class
8. Strengths and Weaknesses		Day 2	Day 2	Week 4	Week 4
8. Script Analysis Exercise		Day 2	Day 2	Week 4	Week 4
8. Beginner Exercise					
8. Intermediate and Advanced Exercise		Day 2	Day 2	Week 5	Week 5
8. Solo Exercise					
9. Friends and Foes	Day 1	Day 2	Day 2	Week 5	Week 5
9. Script Analysis Exercise		Day 2	Day 2	Week 5	Week 5
9. Beginner Exercise					
9. Intermediate and Advanced Exercise		Day 2	Day 2	Week 6	Week 6
9. Solo Exercise					
10. Tools		Day 2	Day 2	Week 6	Week 6
10. Script Analysis Exercise		Day 2	Day 2	Week 6	Week 6
10. Beginner Exercise					
10. Intermediate and Advanced Exercise			Day 3	Week 7	Week 7
10. Solo Exercise					
11. Setting the Scene					Week 8
11. Script Analysis Exercise					Week 8
11. Beginner Exercise					
11. Intermediate and Advanced Exercise					Week 8
11. Solo Exercise					
12. Populating the Scene					Week 9
12. Introduction					Week 9
12. Script Analysis Exercise					Week 9
12. Beginner Exercise					
12. Intermediate and Advanced Exercise					Week 9
12. Solo Exercise					
13. Crafting the Line			Day 4	Week 7	Week 10
13. Script Analysis Exercise			Day 4	Week 7	Week 10
13. Beginner Exercise					
13. Intermediate and Advanced Exercise					
13. Solo Exercise					
14. From Line to Line			Day 4	Week 7	Week 10
14. Script Analysis Exercise			Day 4	Week 7	Week 10
14. Beginner Exercise					
14. Intermediate and Advanced Exercise			Day 4	Week 8	Week 11
14. Solo Exercise					

INTERMEDIATE

Course and Workshop Suggestions	1-Day Workshop	2-Day Workshop	5-Day Workshop	10-Week Class	15-Week Class
15. Focusing the Scene			Day 4	Week 8	Week 11
15. Script Analysis Exercise				Week 8	Week 11
15. Beginner Exercise					
15. Intermediate and Advanced Exercise			Day 4	Week 9	Week 11
15. Solo Exercise					
16. Keeping Everyone in the Scene			Day 5		
16. Script Analysis Exercise					
16. Beginner Exercise					
16. Intermediate and Advanced Exercise			Day 5		
16. Solo Exercise					
17. Maneuvering Through the Scene			Day 5	Week 9	Week 12
17. Script Analysis Exercise				Week 9	Week 12
17. Beginner Exercise					
17. Intermediate and Advanced Exercise			Day 5	Week 10	Week 12
17. Solo Exercise					
18. Ending the Scene			Day 5	Week 10	Week 13
18. Script Analysis Exercise			Day 5	Week 10	Week 13
18. Beginner Exercise					
18. Intermediate and Advanced Exercise			Day 5		Week 13
18. Solo Exercise					
19. Rewriting the Scene					Week 14
19. In the Audience's Shoes					Week 14
19. Voices					Week 14
19. Interactions					Week 14
19. The World					Week 14
19. Forces at Work					Week 14
19. Turning Points					Week 14
19. The Ending					Week 14
20. Scene to Script					Week 15
20. Script Analysis Exercise					Week 15
20. Beginner Exercise					
20. Intermediate and Advanced Exercise					
20. Solo Exercise					

ADVANCED

Course and Workshop Suggestions	1-Day Workshop	2-Day Workshop	5-Day Workshop	10-Week Class	15-Week Class
1. Capturing the Voice					
1. Script Analysis Exercise					
1. Beginner Exercise					
1. Intermediate and Advanced Exercise					
1. Solo Exercise					
2. Imitating the Voice					
2. Script Analysis Exercise					
2. Beginner Exercise					
2. Intermediate and Advanced Exercise					
2. Solo Exercise					
3. Creating an Original Voice					Week 1
3. Script Analysis Exercise					Week 1
3. Beginner Exercise					
3. Intermediate and Advanced Exercise					Week 1
3. Solo Exercise					
4. Status	Day 1	Day 1	Day 1	Week 1	Week 2
4. Script Analysis Exercise					
4. Beginner Exercise					
4. Intermediate and Advanced Exercise					
4. Solo Exercise					
5. Give and Take	Day 1	Day 1	Day 1	Week 1	Week 2
5. Script Analysis Exercise					
5. Beginner Exercise					
5. Intermediate and Advanced Exercise					
5. Solo Exercise					
6. Building Dialogue	Day 1	Day 1	Day 1	Week 1	Week 2
6. Script Analysis Exercise					
6. Beginner Exercise					
6. Intermediate and Advanced Exercise	Day 1	Day 1	Day 1	Week 1	Week 2
6. Solo Exercise					
7. Dialogue on Shifting Sands	Day 1	Day 1	Day 1	Week 2	Week 3
7. Script Analysis Exercise	Day 1	Day 1	Day 1	Week 2	Week 3
7. Beginner Exercise					
7. Intermediate and Advanced Exercise	Day 1	Day 1	Day 1	Week 2	Week 3
7. Solo Exercise					

ADVANCED

Course and Workshop Suggestions	1-Day Workshop	2-Day Workshop	5-Day Workshop	10-Week Class	15-Week Class
8. Strengths and Weaknesses	Day 1	Day 1	Day 1	Week 2	Week 3
8. Script Analysis Exercise	Day 1	Day 1	Day 1	Week 2	Week 3
8. Beginner Exercise					
8. Intermediate and Advanced Exercise					
8. Solo Exercise					
9. Friends and Foes	Day 1	Day 1	Day 1	Week 3	Week 4
9. Script Analysis Exercise					
9. Beginner Exercise					
9. Intermediate and Advanced Exercise				Week 3	Week 4
9. Solo Exercise					
10. Tools	Day 1	Day 1	Day 1	Week 3	Week 4
10. Script Analysis Exercise	Day 1	Day 1	Day 1	Week 3	Week 4
10. Beginner Exercise					
10. Intermediate and Advanced Exercise				Week 4	Week 5
10. Solo Exercise					
11. Setting the Scene			Day 2		Week 6
11. Script Analysis Exercise					Week 6
11. Beginner Exercise					
11. Intermediate and Advanced Exercise			Day 2		Week 6
11. Solo Exercise					
12. Populating the Scene			Day 2		Week 7
12. Introduction			Day 2		Week 7
12. Script Analysis Exercise					
12. Beginner Exercise			Day 2		
12. Intermediate and Advanced Exercise					Week 7
12. Solo Exercise					
13. Crafting the Line		Day 2	Day 2	Week 4	Week 8
13. Script Analysis Exercise					
13. Beginner Exercise					
13. Intermediate and Advanced Exercise					
13. Solo Exercise					
14. From Line to Line		Day 2	Day 2	Week 4	Week 8
14. Script Analysis Exercise		Day 2	Day 2	Week 4	Week 8
14. Beginner Exercise					
14. Intermediate and Advanced Exercise		Day 2	Day 2		Week 8
14. Solo Exercise					

ADVANCED

Course and Workshop Suggestions	1-Day Workshop	2-Day Workshop	5-Day Workshop	10-Week Class	15-Week Class
15. Focusing the Scene		Day 2	Day 3	Week 4	Week 9
15. Script Analysis Exercise					
15. Beginner Exercise					
15. Intermediate and Advanced Exercise				Week 5	Week 9
15. Solo Exercise					
16. Keeping Everyone in the Scene		Day 2	Day 3		Week 9
16. Script Analysis Exercise					Week 9
16. Beginner Exercise					
16. Intermediate and Advanced Exercise			Day 3		
16. Solo Exercise					
17. Maneuvering Through the Scene		Day 2	Day 3	Week 5	Week 10
17. Script Analysis Exercise			Day 3	Week 5	Week 10
17. Beginner Exercise					
17. Intermediate and Advanced Exercise		Day 2	Day 3	Week 6	Week 10
17. Solo Exercise					
18. Ending the Scene		Day 2	Day 3	Week 6	Week 11
18. Script Analysis Exercise		Day 2	Day 3	Week 6	Week 11
18. Beginner Exercise					
18. Intermediate and Advanced Exercise		Day 2	Day 4	Week 7	Week 11
18. Solo Exercise					
19. Rewriting the Scene			Day 5	Week 7	Week 12
19. In the Audience's Shoes			Day 5	Week 9	Week 13
19. Voices					Week 12
19. Interactions			Day 5	Week 7	Week 12
19. The World			Day 5		Week 12
19. Forces at Work			Day 5	Week 8	Week 13
19. Turning Points			Day 5	Week 8	Week 13
19. The Ending			Day 5	Week 8	Week 13
20. Scene to Script				Week 10	Week 14
20. Script Analysis Exercise				Week 10	Week 14
20. Beginner Exercise					
20. Intermediate and Advanced Exercise					Week 15
20. Solo Exercise					

Design-Your-Own Schedule	Syllabus Schedule
1. Capturing the Voice	
1. Script Analysis Exercise	
1. Beginner Exercise	
1. Intermediate and Advanced Exercise	
1. Solo Exercise	
2. Imitating a Voice	
2. Script Analysis Exercise	
2. Beginner Exercise	
2. Intermediate and Advanced Exercise	
2. Solo Exercise	
3. Creating an Original Voice	
3. Script Analysis Exercise	
3. Beginner Exercise	
3. Intermediate and Advanced Exercise	
3. Solo Exercise	
4. Status	
4. Script Analysis Exercise	
4. Beginner Exercise	
4. Intermediate and Advanced Exercise	
4. Solo Exercise	
5. Give and Take	
5. Script Analysis Exercise	
5. Beginner Exercise	
5. Intermediate and Advanced Exercise	
5. Solo Exercise	
6. Building Dialogue	
6. Script Analysis Exercise	
6. Beginner Exercise	
6. Intermediate and Advanced Exercise	
6. Solo Exercise	
7. Dialogue on Shifting Sands	
7. Script Analysis Exercise	
7. Beginner Exercise	
7. Intermediate and Advanced Exercise	
7. Solo Exercise	

Design-Your-Own Schedule	Syllabus Schedule
8. Strengths and Weaknesses	
8. Script Analysis Exercise	
8. Beginner Exercise	
8. Intermediate and Advanced Exercise	
8. Solo Exercise	
9. Friends and Foes	
9. Script Analysis Exercise	
9. Beginner Exercise	
9. Intermediate and Advanced Exercise	
9. Solo Exercise	
10. Tools	
10. Script Analysis Exercise	
10. Beginner Exercise	
10. Intermediate and Advanced Exercise	
10. Solo Exercise	
11. Setting the Scene	
11. Script Analysis Exercise	
11. Beginner Exercise	
11. Intermediate and Advanced Exercise	
11. Solo Exercise	
12. Populating the Scene	
12. Introduction	
12. Script Analysis Exercise	
12. Beginner Exercise	
12. Intermediate and Advanced Exercise	
12. Solo Exercise	
13. Crafting the Line	
13. Script Analysis Exercise	
13. Beginner Exercise	
13. Intermediate and Advanced Exercise	
13. Solo Exercise	
14. From Line to Line	
14. Script Analysis Exercise	
14. Beginner Exercise	
14. Intermediate and Advanced Exercise	

Design-Your-Own Schedule	Syllabus Schedule
14. Solo Exercise	
15. Focusing the Scene	
15. Script Analysis Exercise	
15. Beginner Exercise	
15. Intermediate and Advanced Exercise	
15. Solo Exercise	
16. Keeping Everyone in the Scene	
16. Script Analysis Exercise	
16. Beginner Exercise	
16. Intermediate and Advanced Exercise	
16. Solo Exercise	
17. Maneuvering Through the Scene	
17. Script Analysis Exercise	
17. Beginner Exercise	
17. Intermediate and Advanced Exercise	
17. Solo Exercise	
18. Ending the Scene	
18. Script Analysis Exercise	
18. Beginner Exercise	
18. Intermediate and Advanced Exercise	
18. Solo Exercise	
19. Rewriting the Scene	
19. In the Audience's Shoes	
19. Voices	
19. Interactions	
19. The World	
19. Forces at Work	
19. Turning Points	
19. The Ending	
20. Scene to Script	
20. Script Analysis Exercise	
20. Beginner Exercise	
20. Intermediate and Advanced Exercise	
20. Solo Exercise	

For Further Reading

After you have mastered the art of dialogue writing, you are ready to move on to writing full-length scripts. Here are a few books that can get you started down this road:

Theater

McLaughlin, Buzz. 1997. *The Playwright's Process.* New York: Back Stage Books.
Spencer, Stuart. 2002. *The Playwright's Guidebook.* New York: Faber & Faber.

Film

Field, Syd. 2005. *Screenplay.* New York: Delta.
Halperin, Michael. 2003. *Writing the Second Act.* Studio City, CA: Michael Wiese Productions.
McKee, Robert. 1997. *Story: Substance, Structure, Style and The Principles of Screenwriting.* New York: Harper Collins.
Snyder, Blake. 2005. *Save the Cat!* Studio City, CA: Michael Wiese Productions.
Vogler, Christopher. 2007. *The Writer's Journey (3rd Ed.).* Studio City, CA: Michael Wiese Productions.

General

Johnstone, Keith. 1987. *Impro.* New York: Routledge/ Theatre Arts Books.

Note

The author acknowledges the authors and copyright owners of the following books, stage plays and
motion pictures from which short excerpts of prose,
dialogue or single frame images have been used in
this book for purposes of commentary, criticism,
and scholarship under the Fair Use Doctrine.

All About Eve, ©1950. Screenplay by Joseph L.
Mankiewicz, Story by Mary Orr. 20th Century-
Fox Home Entertainment, All Rights Reserved.

As Good As It Gets, ©1998. Screenplay by Mark
Andrus and James L. Brooks. Columbia TriStar
Home Entertainment, All Rights Reserved.

Biography, @1952. Stage play by S. N. Behrman,
Published in *4 Plays By S. N. Behrman: The Second
Man, Biography, Rain from Heaven, End of Summer*,
New York: Random House. All Rights Reserved.

Casablanca, ©2005. Screenplay by Julius J. Epstein,
Philip G. Epstein and Howard Koch, based on the
play *Everybody Comes to Rick's* by Murray Burnett
and Joan Alison. Warner Home Video, All Rights
Reserved.

The Emperor Brutus Jones, ©1921. Stage Play by
Eugene O'Neill. Published in *Eugene O'Neill:
Complete Plays 1913-1920*, New York: Library of
America, All Rights Reserved.

Fight Club, ©2000. Screenplay by Jim Uhls, Novel by Chuck Palahniuk. 20th Century-Fox Home Entertainment, All Rights Reserved.

Goodfellas, ©2006, Screenplay by Nicholas Pileggi & Martin Scorsese. Warner Home Video, All Rights Reserved.

Gone With the Wind, ©2005. Screenplay by Sidney Howard, Novel by Margaret Mitchell, Warner Home Video, All Rights Reserved.

Grace, ©2008. Stage play by Mick Gordon and A.C. Grayling, London: Oberon Books, All Rights Reserved.

The Graduate, ©1999. Screenplay by Calder Willingham and Buck Henry, novel by Charles Webb. MGM Home Entertainment, All Rights Reserved.

Hamlet ©2007. Screenplay by Kenneth Branaugh. Stage play by William Shakespeare. Warner Home Video, All Rights Reserved.

His Girl Friday ©1940. Screenplay by Charles Lederer, stage play *The Front Page* by Ben Hecht and Charles MacArthur. Columbia Pictures.

The Jazz Singer, ©2007. Adaptation by Alfred A. Cohn, stage play by Samson Raphaelson. Warner Home Video, All Rights Reserved.

King John, stage play by William Shakespeare, distributed by Project Guttenberg.*

Life on the Mississippi, by Mark Twain, Distributed by Project Guttenberg.*

The Real Thing, ©2000. Stage play by Tom Stoppard, London: Faber & Faber, All Rights Reserved.

Rosencrantz & Guildenstern Are Dead, ©1967. Stage play by Tom Stoppard, New York: Grove Press, All Rights Reserved.

The Power Outage, ©1985. Stage play by David Mamet, Published in *Goldberg Street: Short Plays and Monologues*, New York: Grove Press, All Rights Reserved.

Proof, ©2006. Screenplay by David Auburn and Rebecca Miller, stage play by David Auburn. The Weinstein Company, All Rights Reserved.

The Search for Signs of Intelligent Life in the Universe, ©1990. Stage play by Jane Wagner, New York: Harper Paperbacks, All Rights Reserved.

The Sea Gull, Stage play by Anton Chekhov. Distributed by Project Guttenberg.*

Sunday in the Park with George, ©1999. Play by James Lapine, music by Stephen Sondheim, inspired by the works of Georges Seurat. Image Entertainment, All Rights Reserved.

Star Wars, ©1977. Screenplay by George Lucas. 20th Century-Fox Film Corporation, All Rights Reserved.

About the Author

Penny Penniston is a Chicago-area playwright and screenwriter. Her newest play, *Spin*, will have its world premiere with Chicago's Theater Wit during the 2009–2010 season.

Previous stage plays include *now then again* and *The Roaring Girl. now then again* had its world premiere in Chicago at the Bailiwick Repertory Theater on February 17, 2000. The show ran for seventeen weeks, received wide critical acclaim, and was awarded Chicago's Joseph Jefferson Citation for "Best New Work." In 2002, *now then again* was published by Broadway Play Publishing.

Penniston coauthored *The Roaring Girl* with her husband, director Jeremy Wechsler. This adaptation of the 1611 comedy by Thomas Middleton and Thomas Dekker had its world premiere in Chicago with Shakespeare's Motley Crew. It received a Joseph Jefferson nomination for "Best Adaptation."

Penniston's screenplays include *Love is Brilliant* (an adaptation of her stage play, *now then again*), *Going*

Out of the Box, and *Gay Pride & Prejudice. Love is Brilliant* received the Sloan Award at the 2005 Tribeca Film Festival.

Penniston has written short plays for Chicago's Collaboraction Theater Company and Shakespeare's Motley Crew. From 2002–2007, she taught playwriting as an adjunct professor in the Theater Department of Northwestern University. She has also guest lectured at DePaul University. For more information on Penniston's work, see her website at *www.peninkent.com.*

THE WRITER'S JOURNEY
3RD EDITION

MYTHIC STRUCTURE FOR WRITERS

CHRISTOPHER VOGLER

BEST SELLER
OVER 170,000 COPIES SOLD!

See why this book has become an international best seller and a true classic. *The Writer's Journey* explores the powerful relationship between mythology and storytelling in a clear, concise style that's made it required reading for movie executives, screenwriters, playwrights, scholars, and fans of pop culture all over the world.

Both fiction and nonfiction writers will discover a set of useful myth-inspired storytelling paradigms (i.e., "The Hero's Journey") and step-by-step guidelines to plot and character development. Based on the work of Joseph Campbell, *The Writer's Journey* is a must for all writers interested in further developing their craft.

The updated and revised third edition provides new insights and observations from Vogler's ongoing work on mythology's influence on stories, movies, and man himself.

"This book is like having the smartest person in the story meeting come home with you and whisper what to do in your ear as you write a screenplay. Insight for insight, step for step, Chris Vogler takes us through the process of connecting theme to story and making a script come alive."
> – Lynda Obst, Producer, *Sleepless in Seattle, How to Lose a Guy in 10 Days;*
>   Author, *Hello, He Lied*

"This is a book about the stories we write, and perhaps more importantly, the stories we live. It is the most influential work I have yet encountered on the art, nature, and the very purpose of storytelling."
> – Bruce Joel Rubin, Screenwriter, *Stuart Little 2, Deep Impact,*
>   *Ghost, Jacob's Ladder*

CHRISTOPHER VOGLER is a veteran story consultant for major Hollywood film companies and a respected teacher of filmmakers and writers around the globe. He has influenced the stories of movies from *The Lion King* to *Fight Club* to *The Thin Red Line* and most recently wrote the first installment of *Ravenskull*, a Japanese-style manga or graphic novel. He is the executive producer of the feature film *P.S. Your Cat is Dead* and writer of the animated feature *Jester Till*.

$26.95 · 300 PAGES · ORDER NUMBER 76RLS · ISBN: 193290736x

SAVE THE CAT!

THE LAST BOOK ON SCREENWRITING YOU'LL EVER NEED

BLAKE SNYDER

BEST SELLER

He's made millions of dollars selling screenplays to Hollywood and now screenwriter Blake Snyder tells all. "Save the Cat" is just one of Snyder's many ironclad rules for making your ideas more marketable and your script more satisfying — and saleable, including:

- The four elements of every winning logline.
- The seven immutable laws of screenplay physics.
- The 10 genres and why they're important to your movie.
- Why your Hero must serve your Idea.
- Mastering the Beats.
- Mastering the Board to create the Perfect Beast.
- How to get back on track with ironclad and proven rules for script repair.

This ultimate insider's guide reveals the secrets that none dare admit, told by a show biz veteran who's proven that you can sell your script if you can save the cat.

"Imagine what would happen in a town where more writers approached screenwriting the way Blake suggests? My weekend read would dramatically improve, both in sellable/producible content and in discovering new writers who understand the craft of storytelling and can be hired on assignment for ideas we already have in house."
  – From the Foreword by Sheila Hanahan Taylor, Vice President,
    Development at Zide/Perry Entertainment, whose films
    include *American Pie, Cats and Dogs* and *Final Destination*

"Want to know how to be a successful writer in Hollywood? The answers are here. Blake Snyder has written an insider's book that's informative — and funny, too."
  – David Hoberman, Producer, *Raising Helen, Walking Tall,*
    Bringing Down the House

"Blake Snyder's Save the Cat! *could also be called* Save the Screenwriter!, *because that's exactly what it will do:* Save the Screenwriter *time,* Save the Screenwriter *frustration, and* Save the Screenwriter's *sanity... by demystifying the Hollywood process."*
  – Andy Cohen, Literary Manager/Producer; President, Grade A Entertainment

BLAKE SNYDER has sold dozens of scripts, including co-writing the Disney hit, *Blank Check,* and *Nuclear Family* for Steven Spielberg — both million-dollar sales.

$19.95 · 216 PAGES · ORDER NUMBER 34RLS · ISBN: 1932907009